LEADING
LEADERS

Books by Aubrey Malphurs

Being Leaders
Building Leaders (coauthor)
Developing a Vision for Ministry in the 21st Century, 2d ed.
Maximizing Your Effectiveness
Planting Growing Churches for the 21st Century, 3d ed.
Pouring New Wine into Old Wineskins
Vision America
Ministry Nuts and Bolts
Strategy 2000
Values-Driven Leadership, 2d ed.
Developing a Dynamic Mission for Your Ministry
Biblical Manhood and Womanhood
Advanced Strategic Planning
The Dynamics of Church Leadership
Doing Church
Next Church (coauthor)
A Contemporary Handbook for Weddings and Funerals and Other Occasions (coauthor)

LEADING
LEADERS

EMPOWERING CHURCH BOARDS
FOR MINISTRY EXCELLENCE

A New Paradigm for Board Leadership

AUBREY
MALPHURS

BakerBooks

Grand Rapids, Michigan

Published by Baker Books
a division of Baker Publishing Group
P.O. Box 6287, Grand Rapids, MI 49516-6287
www.bakerbooks.com

Printed in the United States of America

Library of Congress Cataloging-in-Publication Data
Malphurs, Aubrey
    Leading leaders : empowering church boards for ministry excellence / Aubrey Malphurs.
        p.   cm.
    Includes bibliographical references and index.
    ISBN 0-8010-9178-0
    1. Church officers. 2. Christian leadership. 3. Church committees. 4. Church management. I. Title.
BV705.M36 2005
253—dc22   2004026954

CONTENTS

111153

INTRODUCTION

There aren't many books on board leadership from a Christian perspective. I know of few. However, leaders and researchers have written a number of books and articles on governance boards from a corporate or business perspective. What does this tell us? Does the business world know something that we don't? Does it recognize the importance of good board governance to the life and productivity of a company more than Christians realize this need for the church? Those of us who have spent time on a church or parachurch board may wonder at such questions, and some of us might snicker a bit. But perhaps this is more a comment on the failure of Christian boards to function well than it is on their importance to ministry and leadership.

As we shall see, usually it is boards, rather than pastors, that lead churches. And if we believe along with Bill Hybels that the church is the hope of the world, and leadership is the hope of the church, then what are we doing to improve leadership at the board level? If the condition of our churches early in the twenty-first century is an indication, the answer is very little.

In North America and Europe we live in what now is generally acknowledged to be a post Judeo-Christian world that is drinking deeply from the fountain of postmodernism. There has been a growing attempt to train new pastors better and retool the veterans to face this challenge. However, little if any attention has been given to those who are actually leading the majority of churches in North America and Europe—the governance boards, which may be called elder boards, deacon boards, trustee boards, and so on. If we're to make a difference in this new century and if God is going to use us to turn things around in the next ten to twenty years, we must train leadership at the board level.

This book is an early step in that direction. As a consultant and trainer, I've spent much time with pastors, churches, and denominations, helping them plan and think strategically and then to incorporate leadership development into their ministry. In practically every situation it's been evident that the board in concert with the pastor is the key to what happens to the church. I've said on numerous occasions, "As the lead pastor goes, so goes the church," and that's true. However, another statement is also true: "As board leadership goes, so goes the church."

Leading Leaders presents a new paradigm for board leadership. I've discovered that there's a much better way for boards to operate than has been the case traditionally, and it doesn't depend on the size of the church. The information here applies to churches of every size—whether small or a megachurch.

Some of the ideas in this book are based on the excellent work of John Carver in his two books *Boards That Make a Difference* and *Reinventing Your Board*, but, most important, this book is based on Scripture. In the chapters that follow I cite many portions of Scripture to support the new paradigm I recommend.

Carver's books promote the policies approach to board governance—I'll say more about this approach later. Carver writes for and works primarily with nonprofit and public organizations not churches. However, I've had a number of boards comment on the value of Carver's work, and they want help in implementing his policies approach in their churches.

This raises the question of whether it's okay for Christians to use ideas developed by those who are not necessarily Christians. My response to this is that it depends. Even non-Christians often stumble on truth. God hasn't revealed himself only to Christians in the Scriptures (special revelation), but because of his common grace, he's revealed himself to non-Christians through general revelation. The entire Bible is true, but not all of God's truth is found in the Bible. (If it were, it would be a huge book, too large to carry around.) Some truth is found in God's creation. That's why unbelievers are without excuse (Psalm 19). Thus I believe that we're wise to research and study what non-Christians have discovered from God's general revelation. But we must do this by running the information through a biblical, theological grid to make sure that it is actually God's revelation and doesn't contradict Scripture in any way.

Church board leadership is deeply theological and must be approached from a biblical as well as a practical perspective. I want you to feel confident about applying what you will read in this book, because it is theologically sound. I recall one governance board of a large church that interviewed me as a possible leadership trainer. They were most interested in Carver and his practical approach but felt they could supply the theological dimension on their own without my help. I hope they did, but I fear that they (like so many others) are so thirsty for the practical that they forget the importance of the theological.

Leading Leaders is my third book in a trilogy on leadership. The first, *Being Leaders*, defines biblical leadership. The second, *Building Leaders* (coauthored with Will Mancini), addresses the development of leaders at every level of the ministry.[1] *Leading Leaders* is for those who actually lead most churches—church boards. The twelve chapters and fourteen appendices of this book say that I'm trying desperately to balance the theoretical with the practical. I want you to apply to your board what you absorb from these twelve chapters. And the appendices of this book are as instructive and helpful as the chapters, so be sure to read them when I refer you to them and as you develop your own board policies.

The questions at the end of the chapters will help you reflect on and discuss the content. I suggest that you read this book along with your governing board and that you use these questions for board discussion.

My deepest appreciation goes to the following fellow board members of my church (Lake Pointe Church), who contributed in so many ways to the writing of this book: Scott Edwards, Ken Hickman, Garen Horton, Steve Stroope, Robert Terry, Bob Walker, Jeff Watters, Dave Williams, and Sandra Stanley.

1

WHO IS LEADING
THE CHURCHES?

Observations of Board Leadership

The common answer to the question, Who is leading the church? is that it's the pastor. After all, he's the one that the typical, established church hires to do the work of the ministry, such as preaching, teaching, conducting funerals and weddings, administering the ordinances, visiting, and so on. Some congregants even believe that God hears his prayers more than he hears theirs. Another answer that is true in some limited situations is that talented, gifted laypeople, who lead various ministries within the church, actually lead the church. Thus it may come as a surprise that in many churches the pastors and gifted lay leaders aren't the ones who are actually leading the church.

The Leadership of Lay Governing Boards

My experience in working with and researching churches across America is that most (90 percent) are small, established ministries that are lay board–led, whereas, some (likely 10 percent) are larger churches that are either board or senior pastor–led.

According to *Faith Communities Today* (the largest survey of churches ever conducted in the United States), at the turn of the century one-half of congregations have fewer than one hundred regularly attending adults and a full quarter of congregations have fewer than fifty regularly participating adults.[1] Probably much the same is true of Western and Eastern European churches, and some are even smaller there.

According to the same survey, less than 10 percent of churches have more than one thousand people, and many of these churches are also board-led. In fact wise senior pastors of larger churches seek and take the counsel of spiritually mature, wise, multitalented board members. An example is Bill Hybels, the pastor of Willow Creek Community Church near Chicago. When I've attended pastor conferences at Willow, I'm amazed how much Hybels looks to his elder board for leadership. He even has them conduct a session on board leadership at his annual leadership conference.

It's important to note that when the typical smaller, established church brings on a new pastor, he doesn't become a leader right away. This may be a conscious or an unconscious decision on the part of the church. The new pastor has to work through several phases—the chaplain, pastor, and leader phases—before becoming a significant leader. As the new pastor successfully works through the phases, he builds credibility (see the chart below). Usually this takes no less than five or six years; however, some churches in general and church boards in particular may never turn the reins of authority over to the pastor, even after he's gone through the phases. Currently, far too many pastors aren't staying around in these churches long enough to find out. Thus these churches are perpetually board run. Consequently, the clear majority of churches in America are led by lay governing boards no matter what polity (church government) they profess.

Pastoral Phases

Phase 1: Chaplain	Phase 2: Pastor	Phase 3: Leader Credibility

Therefore, the weight of leadership in the vast majority of churches in North America and beyond lies as much with the governing board as with the pastor. Yet, though most boards are well intentioned, most have not been trained for their work and most have not thought through or fully understood what they're doing. This lack of training and understanding means that most boards do not function well.

As we move into the twenty-first century, more churches and seminaries are addressing the need to better prepare pastors as leaders, and more churches are beginning to train their lay leaders to guide their ministries within the church. However, few if any are training their lay leadership boards. Bill Hybels is correct when he observes that the church is the hope of the world, and leadership is the hope of the church. But it will take more, much more, than the training of pastors, their staff, and their lay leaders of ministries to correct the current church crisis that exists in so many parts of our world.

There is a huge need to train church governing boards to function better as leaders of leaders, because, in the majority of churches, they are in influential leadership positions, even more than the pastors. As the title of this book suggests, they are potentially the leaders of leaders. In fact it is likely that they are the key to the revitalization of the church in the twenty-first century.

Unfortunately, even those who are at the leading edge of thinking about church leadership appear to have missed this obvious but crucial

The weight of leadership in the vast majority of churches in North America and beyond lies as much with the governing board as with the pastor.

point. In my consulting and training ministry, however, I sense a growing grassroots interest in a fresh approach to board governance. Within the last few months I've met or been contacted by several representatives of church boards that are tired of the old board-business-as-usual paradigm. They want to know what books are available on this topic. They desire high-impact leadership training so they can work with, not against, the senior pastor and make a deep, lasting spiritual impression on their lost and dying community. They don't realize they need a new

In my consulting and training ministry, I sense a growing grassroots interest in a fresh approach to board governance.

paradigm for board leadership. Now is the time for such a paradigm, and it's the purpose of this book to provide one that focuses on policy governance within a biblically based context.

The Performance of Lay Boards

The General State of the Church

Are lay boards leading churches well? A look at the general state of the church reveals that they are not. In the early twenty-first century, far too many churches are either plateaued or dying. Randy Frazee and Lyle Schaller write that "66–75 percent of congregations founded before 1960 are plateaued or shrinking."[2]

Win Arn, a church growth research expert, contrasts the state of the church at the end of the twentieth century with that of the 1950s. He writes, "In the years following World War II thousands of new churches were established. Today, of the approximately 350,000 churches in America, four out of five are either plateaued or declining."[3] And Thom Rainer writes: "Only one person is reached for Christ every year for every eighty-five church members in America."[4]

George Barna comments on the church's need for leaders: "I have reached several conclusions regarding the future of the Christian Church in America. The central conclusion is that the American church is dying due to a lack of strong leadership. In this time of unprecedented opportunity and plentiful resources, the church is actually losing influence. The primary reason is the lack of leadership. Nothing is more important than leadership."[5]

The Functioning of the Boards

If we look at the governing boards themselves, we find that they are not functioning well. In one place, board expert and consultant John Carver describes governing boards as "incompetent groups made up of competent people." In another place he calls them "mindful people regularly carrying out mindless activity" and "intelligent people tied up in trivia."[6] Phillip Jenkins calls them "the well-intentioned in full pursuit of the irrelevant."[7]

Peter Drucker describes corporate boards: "There is one thing that all boards have in common, regardless of their legal position. They do not function. The decline of the board is a universal phenomenon of this century."[8]

Again, Carver says, "In my experience, *most* of what the majority of boards do either does not need to be done or is a waste of time when done by the board. Conversely, most of what boards need to do for strategic leadership is not done."[9]

These are descriptions of boards in general. My experience is that it's the same or worse in the congregational world. George Babbes writes: "It's no secret that most ministries are not managed well. . . . Few ministry boards seem to understand what really drives the ministry's effectiveness and fewer still can evaluate progress toward ministry objectives."[10] Even those that excel on boards in the corporate context often struggle in the congregational context. If corporate boards struggle with managing trivia, the congregational boards even more so: "When will we have our next pot luck?" "Somebody needs to take an extra turn in the nursery next week." "Who's going to mow the lawn?" and so on. When you challenge a church board's culture, the response is, "We've always done it that way" or "That's the way we do things around here."

In *Nailing Down a Board* Charles Ryrie, a veteran of many different kinds of Christian boards, writes: "It has been said that boards seem to have one thing in common—they do not function well, or when they do function, it is at a low percentage of their potential."[11] Later in the same book he tells the following story: "During a short break in a board meeting I was attending some years ago, one of the other board members turned to me and asked what I did to relieve the boredom of that meeting. Mind you, this was an annual meeting and one would expect that a number of important matters would be up for serious discussion. But it was boring—no question about it. I don't recall my reply, but I recall this, he said that, since he was a pastor, he was spending the time memorizing the middle verses of hymns!"[12]

Recently one of my teaching associates at Dallas Seminary reflected on his experience as a board member. He described it as "sitting in an elders' meeting until the early hours, debating the color of the hymnal." He didn't literally mean this. However, it was the picture he chose to reflect the incompetence of his church's board. He saw it as a waste of his time.

In my training and consulting ministry, I've worked with a number of churches over the years, and my experience is that few have effective, functional boards. In fact I can't name five churches with healthy, functioning boards. The problem in general is that both the boards and pastors don't know how to function in a governance relationship. Seminaries don't train pastors in board governance, and laypeople are seldom exposed to such an approach, even those in the corporate world. Thus most churches rely on board tradition—how they've done it in the past—"the way we do things around here." Some may borrow from another church or do it the way they did in the last church. The problem with this is that each church has a different culture and what may (or may not) work for one doesn't necessarily work for the other. And to compound the problem, boards and the committees that are supposed to serve them can harbor power people who attempt to take control and run the church the way they think is best.

Your Church Board

The important question for you to consider is not how other boards are doing but rather how *your* board is doing. If your board functions like most, the answer is not well.

A senior pastor of a large denominational church in the Midwest confided in me recently: "I hate board meetings!" However, I suspect that he wouldn't admit this to the other board members. And the irony is that the others probably hate board meetings as well, yet they won't admit it either. Someone needs to blow the whistle on poor, ineffective board meetings.

Before reading any further, if you're a pastor, turn to the board audit in appendix A. You and your board members should take the audit. If you are a board member in a church without a pastor, take the audit

---

Someone needs to blow the whistle on poor, ineffective board meetings.

---

to see how you're doing. It's imperative that those who take the audit be truthful. Your answers should reflect how things really are, not how you want them to be. I'm not implying that you would lie, but there is often a tendency to "fudge" a little, so that the board looks better than it is. It's important that you discourage this kind of response if you really want to get at the truth.

After the board takes the audit, discuss the results. You may want to ask the board members: "Given a viable option, such as another ministry in the church, would you still choose to be involved on the board?" The responses will tell you a lot about how your board is doing.

What's the Problem?

The Function

The primary problem that is the root cause of a board's struggles is its understanding of its function or fundamental role as a governing group. What is the board supposed to be doing? This is the board function issue.

The problem essentially is very simple. Boards don't understand their role or how they are to function. Most perpetuate the functions of the past. New members come on board and observe the culture of the current board and the role it plays. They become enculturated, function the same way, and the situation perpetuates itself, usually without challenge.

Few if any boards ever pause long enough in the midst of their business to examine and discuss their role. Fewer still ever consider whether their current role is best for the church's present situation, which could be a new pastor, a numerical growth spurt, numerical decline, as well as other situations. And fewer still change their roles when their situation changes.

The Process

Another problem is the board process. The board function issue asks, What is this board supposed to be doing? The board process issue asks, How is it supposed to conduct its business? The current board process paradigm is a major culprit. Following are some board process problems. As you read through them, circle, at least mentally, any that apply to your situation.

Limited meeting time. Unlike full-time staff, boards don't have enough time to deal with all the business on their agenda, much of which is often trivial. Consequently, boards meet for long hours but still don't get everything done. They may spend time debating the mundane and never get around to what's truly important. Often there is little time given to meaningful discussion of major, challenging, strategic ministry matters. Limited meeting time is at the top of most board lists of board process problems.

Trivial agenda items. Between board meetings, the traditional board collects agenda items from all sorts of people: some outside the congregation, most within it, such as staff, senior pastors, and board members. While someone may screen items, most boards feel obligated to deal with the majority of them. This results in far too much trivia getting through, so that the board deals mostly with insignificant issues and never gets around to the most important ones. Often boards deal with issues they have no business deciding and fail to deal with major strategic issues that they should decide.

Inconsistent decision making. The typical board makes event decisions. As it deals with the various issues that pass before it, it makes decisions based on how the board members feel about the issue currently in the church's history. This may result in later decisions that are arbitrary and inconsistent. For example, a board makes a decision on an agenda item. A few years later, the same or similar board makes a decision on a related item, without realizing it contradicts the former decision.

Unclear lines of authority. Boards fail to clarify the lines of authority between themselves, committees, board members, the senior pastor, and the staff. Sometimes they give too much authority to a single board person to whom the others look when making decisions. This tends to result in turf struggles that the senior pastor usually loses.

Adverse board interference. Well-intentioned boards and board members often interfere with the senior pastor's and staff's ministries, such as when they attempt to micromanage the church. The problem is that the typical board rarely has the expertise to advise the professional staff on how they should conduct their ministries. Also this interference has an adverse effect on staff esprit de corps and on trust between board members and staff.

Unclear board expectations. Most board members have certain expectations for the pastor and staff, based on the church's tradition (how they or others have functioned in the past). And these expectations have been known to conflict with one another. The problem is that often the pastor and staff don't know what the expectations are. Another related problem is that the boundaries between the pastor's business and the board's business aren't clearly defined, resulting in the board encroaching on and even micromanaging the pastor's business, or the pastor trespassing on what has traditionally been the board's territory.

Low esprit de corps. When board members feel that their meetings are a waste of time and that the board isn't accomplishing anything significant for the ministry, they don't look forward to meetings and often skip them. The members feel that they are performing below their leadership potential. Good leaders don't function well when they perceive that they are pursuing incompetence in the midst of trivia. Eventually, they politely resign their position to find better things to do for God with their time.

Cultural conditioning. New board members have the potential to bring fresh, objective ideas to the board or ask thought-provoking, even probing, questions that positively challenge the prevailing status quo. I've been on at least one board where, wonderfully, this took place. The result is that one new member helped the rest of us think long and hard about what we were doing and why we were doing it. However, this is rare. When a person joins any board, there are a number of cultural forces at play. Each new member is joining a group with unwritten rules and already established norms (do's and don'ts). He or she quickly learns that it's easier to go along with the others than to risk trying to change things. Asking cogent questions or raising objections in the face of so-called experienced opinions or the prevailing mind-set risks invoking mild displeasure at best or incurring other members' wrath at worse.

Poor planning. Some board leaders don't know how to plan their meetings. They may be wonderful visionaries and powerful motivators, but they lack basic knowledge or skills in planning. Others, even with some degree of knowledge or skill, find they don't have the time to plan well. In either case, meetings are poorly planned, as evidenced by the length of the meetings and the little that is ultimately accomplished in them.

Too many participants. Some churches—both small and large—have too many members on their boards. Old First Church, for example, may have anywhere from twenty-five to fifty deacons on its board. Not much is accomplished on such a large board. However, smaller churches can experience the same problem, thinking that bigger is better. Where there is a large number of board participants, vital give-and-take about the issues that are most important to the ministry is limited. Also, if some of the members are vocal, dissatisfied people, they can so preoccupy the board with their complaints that it never gets to its agenda.

Focus on the past. Boards often have a tendency to focus on the past or the recent present rather than on future ministry challenges and opportunities. Focusing on or ministering in the past is much like driving a car by looking in the rearview mirror rather than out the front windshield at the road ahead. It's important that we learn from the past, but we must not live in the past. The church's vital mission and vision, which are ultimately the board's responsibility, are all about the church's future not its past. Paul writes, "But one thing I do: Forgetting what is behind and straining toward what is ahead, I press on toward the goal to win the prize for which God has called me heavenward in Christ Jesus" (Phil. 3:13–14).

Board Process Problems

Limited meeting time

Trivial agenda items

Inconsistent decision making

Unclear lines of authority

Adverse board interference

Unclear board expectations

Low esprit de corps

Cultural conditioning

Poor planning

Too many participants

Focus on the past

The Training

Not only are the board's function and process faulty, but no one is training or developing church board members, especially new board members, to lead well in board contexts. This is the third problem for a church board's struggles and precipitates the leadership crisis in the church. James Bolt writes: "I contend that this leadership crisis is in reality a *leadership development* crisis. It is this development crisis that leads me to agree that our leaders are 'missing in action.'"[13]

I believe that the reason we don't train people for board leadership has to do with our assumptions. We don't even consider that we don't know what we're doing or that the traditional approach might not be the best. But the ineffectiveness of most boards reveals that something is wrong. Even if we recognize that our boards need training, often we don't know how to do the training. Serving on a leadership board is a unique ministry that calls for special training, but most leadership boards are clueless about this need.

The Board Members

Some argue that the people on the boards are the primary problem. This is correct in some cases. No church in general and no board of leaders in particular are any better than the people who comprise them. For example, some boards are made up of "good old boys," people who have been around for a long time and are willing to attend meetings and express their opinions. Often these people are not spiritually qualified for such leadership and don't know how to lead. Such a board is doomed to failure from the very start.

Another argument is there aren't enough leaders in the churches. This may be true in some churches, but God hasn't withheld the leadership gift from twenty-first century churches in general. Gifted "in-house" leaders tend to move away from struggling, dying ministries that are trying to preserve the past. They move toward ministries where they believe they can exert the greatest impact for the Savior. And I'm not sure this is wrong, especially in situations where churches refuse to change. Nonetheless, many churches are losing some of their best leaders and must take steps to stop this leadership hemorrhaging.

What's the Solution?

Enough of the doom and gloom stuff. What's the solution? A big part of the solution to any problem is discovering and then accurately articulating the problem. When we do this well, the solution becomes obvious. That's why we have to take the time to look at the gloom and doom stuff. The solution here is fourfold.

Determine Proper Board Functions

First, this book will challenge your board to pause and examine its current functions. You must ask, What are we doing; how are we currently functioning as a board; what is our present role? Then you must ask, What should we be doing; what could or should be our function? In chapter 7 I present four primary functions and four occasional roles of church boards.

Find a Better Board Process

The solution to a board's ineffectiveness involves finding a better board process, that is, a much better way to do board ministry. If we want a board to do its job, we must give it a structure in which it can be effective. Until this happens, any board training perpetuates the old paradigm, and that ultimately defeats the whole board ministry process. The answer isn't to redouble our efforts at the same old process or to tinker with that process. The answer is in a whole new way of doing board business. This will take a major paradigm shift. And the purpose of a significant portion of this book is to present such a new paradigm for the unique role of board leadership—one that involves leading leaders with excellence.

Train the Board in the Process

The third part of the solution involves board training. But not just any kind of training will do; it must be the right kind of training. This entails the initial orientation of all new board members as well as that of existing members in how to implement and work the new paradigm process. To have a better process isn't enough. Your new and established leaders must be trained in how to use the process most effectively to accomplish better board leadership. The rest of this book will flesh out both solutions—establishing the new process and then training people in it.

Recruit the Best Board Members

The solution to problem people on the board is to recruit better board leaders. But how do you do that? The key lies in implementing the first three parts of the solution already given. When you determine what your board should be doing, find and implement a better board process, and train those board people in the process, the result will likely be better board people. Word gets around. Quality leaders shy away from bad boards, especially those packed with spiritually unqualified good old boys or good old girls. However, quality leaders are attracted to properly functioning boards with carefully thought-through processes led by spiritually mature people who want to have serious, spiritual impact in their ministry communities.

Questions for Reflection and Discussion

1. Who do you think is leading the majority of churches in North America, the church boards or pastors? Do you agree with the author? Why or why not?
2. Does the governing board or the pastor lead your church? How well is the board or the pastor leading?
3. If your church isn't doing well, and most aren't, what do you think is the problem?
4. Which of the eleven board process problems identified in this chapter apply to your church situation?
5. Have your church board members received any training to serve on a board? Why or why not?

2

THE GOVERNING BOARD
A Definition of Board Leadership

Before I go any further, I need to provide a definition of a governing board so that we know what it is we're talking about. Essentially, there are two kinds of boards. Advisory boards and governing boards. An *advisory board* is just what its name implies. It serves to advise and has no authority to exercise any power. I encourage church plants that insist on having a board to begin with an advisory board as a precursor to a governing board (it allows time for spiritual,

---

A governing board is a gathering of two or more wise, spiritually qualified leaders.

---

mature leadership to emerge). And that's all that I'll say about advisory boards. The rest of the book focuses on governing boards.

I define a *governing board* as a gathering of two or more wise, spiritually qualified leaders who have been entrusted with authority to use their power to direct the affairs of the church. (This isn't based on a biblical definition of a governing board, as you'll see below. Scripture doesn't provide us with such a definition.) Let's break this definition down into its individual components.

Size of the Board

Often people ask how large a board should be. Scripture doesn't prescribe board leadership and therefore doesn't dictate the size of a board. I'm aware of some old First Churches that have as many as forty to sixty deacons on their governing boards. John Carver advises, "There is no one right number for board size, but try to keep the board small! The bigger the board, the less likely it is to be businesslike and disciplined. Have a good reason if you want to make it bigger than seven."[1] In light of Carver's advice, it's interesting that in Acts 6:5–6 the Jerusalem church chose seven men to handle a problem for an organization that was well over eight thousand people in size (see Acts 2:41, 47; 4:4).

Church consultant Lyle Schaller advises that just because a church grows larger doesn't mean that it should increase the size of its governing board. Small boards function better than large boards.[2] I attend and serve as an elder on the governing board at Lake Pointe Church in Rockwall, Texas. It's a megachurch of six to seven thousand weekend attenders and operates quite well with only seven elders on its governing board.

In *Back to the Drawing Board*, Colin Carter and Jay Lorsch advise: "Boards should be as small as feasible."[3] Later they write: "We remain strongly committed to the proposition that boards should strive to be as small as they can be. What do we mean by 'small'? If pushed to offer a number, we would suggest a maximum of ten directors. We believe eight to ten members are appropriate for some companies, and even fewer—perhaps six to eight—are sufficient for smaller or less complex companies."[4]

Why the small number? There are several reasons. First, a small number of leaders will be able to interact with one another and then make good decisions. Second, there's more room for give-and-take as well as meaningful discussion. Third, crowded boardrooms exhaust time constraints. On the one hand, many people would like to speak, either to ask questions or make comments. On the other hand, they feel inhibited by the number of people and don't want to take up valuable time. Fourth, small boards have the potential to make better use of the board members' limited time.

Often it's advisable to have an odd number of board members, such as seven. An odd number enables boards to avoid voting ties that could prevent them from moving forward on important decisions.

Leaders on the Board

One former student whom I trained as a church planter and who has been very successful in terms of church growth, once told me that he didn't want leaders on his governing board, because it's sometimes harder to lead leaders than it is to lead followers. While this may be true of traditional boards, it's not true of policy governance boards. With the policy governance approach, you have the potential for leaders to effectively lead leaders in the right way.

Qualifications for Leaders

Not just anybody should serve on a governing board. Again, some churches make the mistake of selecting good old boys or girls for their boards, hoping that they'll preserve the status quo, regardless of their spiritual maturity. Scripture stresses that leaders in ministry must have spiritual qualifications (for example, Acts 6:3–5; 1 Tim. 3:1–10; Titus 1:5–9; 1 Peter 5:1–3). Each church must determine the qualifications that apply to its board. The following summarize spiritual qualifications, based on 1 Timothy 3:1–10 and other similar passages.

1. In general the leader must be "above reproach," that is, he or she has a good reputation among the people. There is nothing that someone could use as an accusation against him or her. This is an overarching qualification that perhaps is a summary of all the rest.
2. If married, the person is the husband of one wife or wife of one husband.
3. He or she is temperate or well balanced, not given to extremes.
4. He or she is sensible, showing good judgment in life and having a proper perspective regarding self and his or her abilities.
5. This person is respectable, God-honoring in all he or she does, so that people have and show respect for him or her.
6. He or she is hospitable, using his or her home as a place to serve and minister to people, whether Christians or non-Christians.
7. He or she is able to teach. When this person teaches the Bible, he or she handles the Scriptures with reasonable skill.

8. If the person drinks alcoholic beverages or engages in other permissible but potentially addictive practices, he or she does so in moderation.

9. This person is never violent and doesn't ever lose control to the point of striking or causing harm to other people or their property.

10. He or she is gentle.

11. He or she is not quarrelsome.

12. This person does not love money and never gives the impression that he or she serves God for material gain.

13. If married with a family, this person manages marriage and the family well.

14. This person is not a recent convert.

15. This person has a good reputation with lost people and those who are not part of the church.

In addition, board members need wisdom for making decisions. Much of what boards do involves decision making, and wisdom along with the Spirit's control is crucial to good decision making (see Acts 6:3 and the book of Proverbs).

In my definition of a governing board, I've used the term *leaders*, and some readers may wonder if this includes both men and women. The issue here is whether women should serve on the board. Essentially

Scripture stresses that leaders in ministry must have spiritual qualifications.

there are two positions. The egalitarian position says that qualified women may serve on the board. Those who hold this view argue that Scripture makes no distinction between persons (men and women) and their functions in the church. A key verse for this position is Galatians 3:28: "There is neither Jew nor Greek, slave nor free, male nor female, for you are all one in Christ Jesus." The complementarian position holds that women should not serve on a governing board. They argue essentially that women are equal to men in essence; however, they are distinct from men in their function or role in the church (1 Cor. 11:1–16; 1 Tim. 2:11–15).

The board of the last church that I pastored held the complementarian position. However, it, like most churches, had more women in attendance than men. We desperately needed the input of women on our board. Consequently, I suggested that there be a women's adviser to the governing board. We adopted this idea and invited an older, spiritually mature woman in our church to serve in this capacity. Regularly we would ask her how the women might feel about a particular policy or action of our all-male board. At times we would excuse her from our meetings, especially if we were dealing with a confidential matter. This worked well for us and might work for you should you be in a church that holds the complementarian position on women in leadership.

Authority of the Board

Every organization has power, whether it wants it or not. In the church we must decide who has the authority to exercise power. The answer depends on the church's polity. The authority may reside in the congregation (congregational polity), in the board (presbyterian polity), in someone outside the church (episcopalian polity), in the senior pastor, the staff, or a church patriarch or matriarch. I'll say more about church polity below.

To exercise power, it is necessary to have authority. It's possible to be in a position of power without the authority to exercise that power. In a church there are several kinds of authority. For example, a pastor may have an "inform and act" authority. In this case the board asks its

---

For spiritually healthy boards to govern well, they must have power.

---

pastor to inform it of a particular action before he acts on it. An "act and inform" authority is when the board allows the pastor to act in a situation but asks that he inform them of that action. The third is an "act" authority. The pastor may act and not necessarily inform anyone, especially if he is acting in his area of leadership, such as staff operations and oversight.

Power is what gets things done. Most often, the congregation or the board itself has entrusted the board, which is usually positioned at the top of the organization, with the authority to exercise power in the affairs of the church. (See appendix J for more about power in relation to pastors and their boards.) For spiritually healthy boards to govern well, they must have power (see Acts 6:2–4).

The Work of a Governing Board

The Savior established churches to accomplish his purpose on earth (see for example, Matt. 16:18; 1 Tim. 3:15). Most churches should opt to use a governing board to direct their affairs in accomplishing their purpose (1 Tim. 5:17). The board accomplishes this best by pursuing its ministry—ministry ends, such as the church's mission and vision—and letting the senior pastor and staff pursue their ministry—ministry means, such as strategy. (I will say more about ministry ends and means later.)

My proposition is that good governance contributes powerfully to the church's corporate spiritual health in a way that glorifies and honors God. And I believe that the way leadership boards can best contribute is mostly through their prayer, monitoring, advice, and involvement in decision making. They will not be involved in all decision making but in major decisions that will affect the ministry's future.

Finally, what really matters is the dedication, energy, time commitment, and skills of the board members, who are committed to and under

A governing board is a gathering of two or more wise, spiritually qualified leaders who have been entrusted with authority to use their power to direct the affairs of the church.

the leadership and lordship of Jesus Christ. Good board leaders will need quality information, robust board discussions, a level of openness, a high degree of transparency, and trust in one another as well as the Savior. I'll say more about these important matters later.

Questions for Reflection and Discussion

1. What is your definition of a governing board? Does it agree or disagree with the author's definition?
2. What is the biblical basis for a church board, if any? What Scripture would you use to justify your position?
3. What is the size of your church's board? Do you think that it's too big, too small, or just about right? Why?

4. Does your board consist of only men or both men and women? Why?

5. Do your board members have to meet spiritual qualifications to be on the board? If not, why not? If so, what are they?

6. In reality, who has the authority in your church to exercise power? Is it the board? Why or why not?

WHY HAVE A
GOVERNING BOARD?
Rationale for Board Leadership

D oes Scripture mandate or prescribe that a church or parachurch
organization have a governing board, such as a board of deacons, elders, or trustees that consists primarily of laypeople
who can participate only part-time?

The Deacon Board

Some people argue that the church should have a board of deacons.
They base this primarily on Acts 6:3–6 and 1 Timothy 3:8–10. However,
there are several problems with this view. First, there is no use of the
term *deacon* in Acts 6:3–6 or anywhere else in the chapter. Also, there
is no evidence here that the apostles were establishing some type of
precedent or setting up a permanent deacon board or any kind of board
that was to be perpetuated in the church.

Second, though 1 Timothy 3:8–10 does refer to a plurality of deacons,
possibly in a church (likely a house church—see below), Paul doesn't

tell us how they functioned. The term *deacon* means servant. Thus we can assume that they served the church in some way, but it isn't stated whether this was as a governance board or in some other role. Therefore, it's evident that Scripture doesn't mandate a deacon board. (Though it's described, it's not prescribed.) Instead, it gives each church the freedom to establish a deacon board if the church desires to function with one.

The Elder Board

Some believe that every church should have a board of lay elders. They argue that many of the elders in the first-century churches were laymen who made up local church leadership boards. They base this on passages that mention a plurality of elders in every church, such as in Acts 14:23; 15:2; 20:17; 1 Timothy 5:17; James 5:14; and also 1 Peter 5:2, which uses the term *overseers*, a synonym for *elders*. (Titus 1:5 and Phil. 1:1 mention a plurality of elders in a city.) They conclude that since the early churches were small, many of these elders must have been part-time leaders or laymen. And the same is true and applies today. Therefore, it's argued that today's churches must have a plurality of leaders (elders) on their boards, or they're not biblical. In addition, the part-time laypeople have as much power and authority to direct the affairs of the church as any full-time staff.

A False Assumption

It was probably not the case that each individual body of the early church had a board of elders. This assumes that the first-century churches were small, like most—80 percent—of today's churches. However, that wasn't the case. They were fairly large churches by today's standards. See the list below.

Note that Luke gives actual numbers for the Jerusalem church in Acts 2:41 ("about three thousand") and 4:4 ("the number of men grew to about five thousand"). Perhaps these figures are key hermeneutically to interpreting or understanding later comments on the growth of the other churches mentioned in Acts where numbers aren't used.

Size of First-Century Churches

The Church in Jerusalem	
Acts 1:15	"numbering about one hundred and twenty"
Acts 2:41	"about three thousand were added to their number"

The Church in Jerusalem *(cont'd.)*

Acts 2:47	"and the Lord added to their number daily"
Acts 4:4	"and the number of men grew to about five thousand"
Acts 5:14	"more men and women believed in the Lord and were added to their number"
Acts 6:1	"the number of disciples was increasing"
Acts 6:7	"The number of disciples in Jerusalem increased rapidly, and a large number of priests became obedient to the faith."

The Church in Judea, Galilee, and Samaria

Acts 9:31	"it [the church] grew in numbers"
Acts 9:35	"All those who lived in Lydda and Sharon saw him and turned to the Lord."
Acts 9:42	"many people believed in the Lord"
Acts 11:21	"a great number of people believed and turned to the Lord"
Acts 11:24	"a great number of people were brought to the Lord"
Acts 11:26	"and taught great numbers of people"

The Church in Iconium

Acts 14:1	"a great number of Jews and Gentiles believed"
Acts 14:21	"and won a large number of disciples"
Acts 16:5	"So the churches . . . grew daily in numbers."

The Church in Thessalonica

Acts 17:4	"Some of the Jews were persuaded and joined Paul and Silas, as did a large number of God-fearing Greeks."

The Church in Berea

Acts 17:12	"Many of the Jews believed, as did also a number of prominent Greek women and many Greek men."

The Church in Corinth

Acts 18:8	"many of the Corinthians who heard him believed and were baptized"
Acts 18:10	"I have many people in this city"

The Church in Ephesus

Acts 19:26	"Paul has convinced . . . large numbers of people here in Ephesus and in practically the whole province of Asia."

The Church in Asia Minor

Acts 21:20	"You see, brother, how many thousands of Jews have believed."

It's likely that many early churches existed and functioned at two levels—the large city church and the smaller house church.

City Churches

The church at Jerusalem met as a large group or city church. (See Acts 2:46; 5:12, 42. Acts 2:41 says there were three thousand people and Acts 4:4 says that later the number of men was five thousand.) The church in Corinth was a city church (compare 1 Cor. 1:2, addressing a city church, with 16:19, which mentions a house church). The church at Ephesus was probably a city church as well (Acts 20:20). The refer-

---

It's likely that many early churches existed and functioned at two levels—the large city church and the smaller house church.

---

ences above to the large size of the churches are probably referring to the city churches. My point here is that these city churches had a plurality of elders—Jerusalem (Acts 15:2) and Ephesus (20:17, 20). See the table below.

House Churches

The city churches met as smaller groups in homes as house churches. This was the case with the church at Jerusalem (Acts 2:46–47; 5:42; 8:3; 12:12–17), Rome (Rom. 16:3–5, 14, 15), Ephesus (Acts 20:20; 1 Cor. 16:19 with Acts 18:24–26), Laodicea (Col. 4:15), and others (Philemon 1–2). It appears that Paul would write a letter to the city church and it would circulate and be read among these house churches. At least this was true of Laodicea (Col. 4:16) and probably Thessalonica (1 Thess. 5:27).

My point here is that the elders were likely the pastors of these smaller house churches. The house churches may have had several, one, or no elders to lead them, depending on the circumstances of each. First Timothy 3:1–10 may indicate that a typical house church, at least in Ephesus, consisted of a single overseer-elder with several helpers (deacons). See the table below.

City Churches and House Churches

Jerusalem	
City Church	Acts 2:46; 5:12, 42; 8:3
House Churches	Acts 2:46–47; 5:42; 8:3; 12:12–17

Ephesus	
City Church	Acts 20:17, 20
House Churches	Acts 20:20; 1 Cor. 16:19 with Acts 18:24–26 (Corinth or Ephesus)

	Corinth
City Church	1 Cor. 1:2; 11:20–22; 14:23; 2 Cor. 1:1
House Churches	1 Cor. 16:19 (Corinth or Ephesus)

Regardless of these examples, Scripture is neither definitive nor prescriptive (only descriptive) on the matter of elders in a church. This is a hermeneutical issue. Nowhere does it say that a church has to have a plurality of elders or that they be part-time leaders or laypeople.

Often the view that the early church had a plurality of lay elders assumes that all first-century churches operated the same way. If one church operated with a plurality of elders, then all must have done so. No evidence exists for this, so it is a non sequitur argument. It would be similar to observing that several Baptist churches in America follow congregational rule; therefore, all Baptist churches in America must and should follow congregational rule. This simply isn't true. And even if there were some evidence that the early churches did have a plurality

---

Nowhere does it say that a church has to have a plurality of elders or that they be part-time leaders or laypeople.

---

of elders, still there is nothing to indicate a mandate saying they had to be organized in this way.

Scripture directs the churches where Timothy ministered to pay their elders—especially those who not only led but taught the Word (1 Tim. 5:17–18). This is a prescriptive passage. To be consistent, shouldn't today's churches pay their lay elders? I don't know of any church that insists on a plurality of elders in every local church that pays all the elders. And some don't even pay the full-time teaching elders. This seems inconsistent.

The Wisdom of Board Leadership

At this point you might assume that I'm against board leadership, but that's not the case. Scripture states that seeking the counsel of others is wise (see the verses from Proverbs below); thus, leading through a governing board of the right people is wise. However, leading with a poor or bad board can be most destructive. The rest of this book will explain the reasons for this.

The Wisdom of Seeking Counsel

Proverbs 11:14	"For lack of guidance a nation falls, but many advisers make victory sure."
Proverbs 15:22	"Plans fail for lack of counsel, but with many advisers they succeed."
Proverbs 20:18	"Make plans by seeking advice; if you wage war, obtain guidance."
Proverbs 24:6	"For waging war you need guidance, and for victory many advisers."

The conclusion of all this is that when Scripture doesn't mandate such a matter, then God gives the local church much freedom to decide on whether to have a governing board, empower it, and determine what it will do. Biblical wisdom seems to favor having such a board and

---

At this point you might assume that I'm against board leadership, but that's not the case.

---

should dictate how that board can best serve each church, considering its unique circumstances. I believe that the policies approach is a wise direction for all churches to pursue.

Questions for Reflection and Discussion

1. How important is it to you to examine what Scripture says about church governance boards?
2. Does Scripture mandate a deacon board? Explain your answer.
3. Does Scripture mandate an elder board? Explain your answer.
4. Why does the author not agree with the traditional position on lay elder boards? Do you agree or disagree? Why?
5. Does the author believe that a church should have a governing board? Why or why not?

4

BOARD ACCOUNTABILITY

Accountability in ministry is critical, because ministry suffers when there are gaps in accountability. In the late twentieth and early twenty-first centuries, a spotlight has been trained on pastoral performance due to all the problems that pastoral leaders have encountered, ranging from sexual sins to financial impropriety. Certainly, pastors must be held accountable for their ministry, and boards too must be held accountable. In the corporate world mismanagement of businesses such as Enron, Tyco, World-Com, and others has also revealed the need for accountability. Board accountability leads to better board governance.

This chapter will explore the two critical accountability questions that every board must answer: To whom is it accountable and for what is it accountable?

Sources of Authority

To whom is the board accountable? I could phrase this question in a different way. I could also ask, Where does the board get its power and the authority to exercise that power? Basically, the answer to either question is the same. This, in essence, is the polity question, and historically there have been three answers. Here I will add a fourth and a fifth possible answer. (I also address these issues in appendix J.)

The Bishops

In some cases the board is accountable to the bishops. This is true in an episcopal form of polity or structure that is hierarchical. It places the authority and thus the power to influence in the hands of bishops who lead outside the individual, local churches. Even if a local church has a governing board, the bishop not the board has the authority to direct the church. Churches that practice this form of government follow a threefold ministry hierarchy, which includes bishops, presbyters, and deacons. Only the bishops have the power to consecrate other bishops and ordain priests and deacons. Thus the bishops hold the power in this system.

There is biblical support for presbyters or elders as well as deacons (1 Tim. 3:1–10 and other passages); however, in Scripture the office of

---

There is biblical support for presbyters or elders as well as deacons.

---

bishop appears to be the same as the office of elder, not a separate office with superior power over the others. Consequently, the episcopal form has little biblical support. This polity is practiced primarily by the Methodist, Orthodox, Anglican, Episcopal, and Roman Catholic churches and by those that are more liturgical in their worship.

The Congregation

In some churches the board is accountable to the congregation. Many churches such as Baptist, Evangelical Free, and some Bible churches profess a congregational polity that says the congregation has the authority to exercise power over the church.

A primary argument for a congregational polity is the priesthood of the believer (1 Peter 2:5, 9). The various descriptive passages that imply that congregations made decisions in certain situations (Acts 6:3, 5; 15:22; 2 Cor. 8:19) also support this view. The congregation's involvement in church discipline (Matt. 18:17; 1 Cor. 5:4–5) is another argument for the board's accountability to the congregation.

There is no way, however, that a congregation can direct or lead a church. So they must give a certain amount of authority and power to a lay governing board (called elders, deacons, trustees, and so forth) to direct them. But final authority supposedly rests with the congregation that votes corporately as a body on various issues that affect the church and the people that make up the board.

In reality the congregation votes on what the board lets them vote on. This ranges anywhere from a plethora of matters in small churches, such as the color of the new carpet, to just a few things in larger churches, such as a new pastor, a building program, or a move to a new location. Consequently, even congregational churches are largely governed by a board.

The Governing Board

A third answer is that the board is accountable only to itself. It's the source of its own power. Presbyterian churches and some Bible churches operate by a federal form of polity where power and the authority to exercise that power is vested in the hands of a board of leaders, often called elders. This is a representative form of government, the board attempting to represent the people or the people governing indirectly through their leaders. Consequently, this model acknowledges and intends that a lay governing board will lead the church.

The Senior Pastor

Some would say that a board should not have authority to exercise any power. Strong, gifted leaders, perhaps the leader who planted the church or the pastor of a large, growing church, often exercise power. This happens when the board or congregation grants authority to the pastor or by default. Thus any power the board has is granted by the senior pastor.

Often these churches have a lay board, but it isn't necessarily a governing board, or if it is, it is accountable to the pastor. It could be an advisory group for the pastor or an accountability group. These churches would not benefit from the model of governance espoused in this book because it primarily addresses the majority of churches that are board-led.

A Patriarch or Matriarch

In some churches the authority to lead is vested in a church patriarch or matriarch. This is very common in small and some larger churches. These men and women are often older, long-tenured members who have garnered the respect of the board as well as the congregation, due to their faithfulness and service to the church.

They may or may not be on the board, but before any major decisions are made, the church consults with these people. If they're on the board, the other board members will read the direction that they're taking. If they're not on the board, some board members will meet with them prior to the board or congregational meeting to get their opinion, which becomes the board's position.

It appears, at least to someone on the outside or fringes of the church, that the board has the authority to make decisions. However, behind the scenes the patriarch or matriarch is usually making the decisions, at least the most important ones. Thus any power the board may have is granted by the patriarch or matriarch.

Sources of Authority

The bishops
The congregation
The governing board
The senior pastor
A patriarch or matriarch

Ministry Accountability

A governing board must know not only *to whom* it is accountable but also *for what* it is accountable. The answer determines the board's core mission or ministry ends and the congregational and staff expectations of the board.

Ministry Means

Ministry means are staff responsibilities that involve determining and implementing the methods (strategy) that accomplish the church's mission. Ministry means call for a staff that has time and ministry expertise, and these staff people must be located on site. A hired ministry staff best accomplishes ministry means.

Ministry Ends

The tasks of determining, assigning, and monitoring the church's mission and vision and the issues surrounding the same comprise ministry ends. The policy governance approach asserts that the board's primary mission is ministry ends–related. Its mission is to see that the church pursues its Christ-given mission. That mission, according to the Savior, is the Great Commission: to make and mature believers at home and abroad (Matt. 28:19–20; Mark 16:15). Making believers is evangelism. Maturing believers is edification. At home and abroad identifies where the church will go and whom it will reach—the Great Commission has geographical implications (Acts 1:8). Consequently, the primary expectation of the governing board is that it define and declare the

The policy governance approach asserts that the board's primary mission is ministry ends–related. Its mission is to see that the church pursues its Christ-given mission.

church's mission as the Great Commission, assign responsibility to a primary leader (the senior pastor) to accomplish the commission, and then monitor the accomplishment of the mission according to agreed on expectations.

The reason that this is the primary responsibility of the board is that senior pastors come and go. Most serve at one church for a while and then move on to other ministries for various reasons. However, most board members have longevity and will be at the church long after a pastor has left it. To assign the mission exclusively to the senior pastor would likely result in diminishing or even the loss of the mission during those times when the church is looking for a senior pastor. Thus it is the board's primary responsibility to be the keepers, promoters, and monitors of the mission and vision of the church, assuring the effectiveness and continuance of the ministry.

The Pastor's Responsibility

One of the primary responsibilities of the senior pastor is to see that the mission is being accomplished. I believe that this is an aspect of what Paul meant in 1 Timothy 5:17 when he described elders as those "who direct the affairs of the church," which involves recruiting and training the best staff possible along with adopting the best methods to see that the church realizes its mission (ministry means). The board must see that the senior pastor accomplishes this.

The reality is that most boards and pastors don't function this way. In some churches the governing board attempts to do the work of the senior pastor and staff (ministry means), which isn't possible (they don't have the time and expertise, and they aren't on site). In other churches the staff is involved in doing the work of the board (ministry ends) by default plus its own work (ministry means), or it's pursuing ministry means and no one is addressing ministry ends. The tragedy of the latter scenario is that the only reason for ministry means to exist is to

---

One of the primary responsibilities of the senior pastor is to see that the mission is being accomplished.

---

accomplish ministry ends. If the ends have not been identified, there is no purpose for the means. A church can't survive long in this mode.

Ministry Accountability in the Church

The Board's Primary Responsibility: Establishing the mission and monitoring its accomplishment (ministry ends)
The Pastor's Primary Responsibility: The accomplishment of the mission (ministry means)

Questions for Reflection and Discussion

1. How important is it that a church's governing board have some kind of accountability? Why? Does yours?
2. To whom do you believe a board should be accountable? Why? Is this true of your board? Why or why not?
3. For what should a board be held accountable? Why? Is this the case with your church? Why or why not?
4. What should be the board's role in your church? What should be the pastor's role? Is this the situation in your church? Why or why not?

5

BOARD COMPOSITION

Now it's time to address the composition of a governing board. When we consider who should be on the governing board, we must consider the qualifications of the desired people and how to select and recruit these people. Then, once they are on the board, how will their progress be monitored?

Governing Board Constituents

There are several different types of constituents of the governing board, and they may each function differently in their role of leader of leaders.

The governing board is made up of people who lead by defining and determining the church's direction (the mission and vision), assigning responsibility to accomplish the mission and vision to a senior pastor, and then monitoring their accomplishment, holding him, not the staff, accountable for this. Along with this responsibility is the development of the policies that guide the board in what they do, what the senior pastor does, and their relationship with him. We'll see in chapter 7 that all of this and more fall under the primary responsibilities of the board and may be described as praying, monitoring, deciding, and advising.

Usually the board members are lay spiritual leaders in the congregation, and the senior pastor is on the board. I advise churches not to have other staff members on the board. The problem is that you want to encourage board leaders to differ with one another at times, and it would be difficult for a staff person to differ with the senior pastor on any issue. Some would refuse to do it, fearing that this would breach their loyalty to their boss or even create an adversarial relationship.

The Senior Pastor

One of the board members is the senior pastor. He is equal to the other board members and is involved in defining and determining the church's mission and vision. He is also an employee of the board and serves it by developing a strategy that accomplishes the mission and vision. He is involved in determining the policies that govern the board, himself, and his relationship to the board.

When the senior pastor retires, he should not stay on the board. This is almost always a bad idea. I would go so far as to argue that he shouldn't even stay at the church, because his presence on the board or in the congregation may weaken the effectiveness of and even intimidate the new pastor. Also many of the people—especially the older members—may look to him for leadership rather than the new senior pastor, and this could be most divisive. For the well-being of the church as well as the board, the former pastor should move to another church on his own initiative.

The Board Chairperson

Many boards will choose a chairperson. He, or in some churches she (see my discussion of the gender of board members in chapter 2), may set the board's agenda, lead the board meetings, interpret the policies governing the board and also its relationship with the senior pastor, and represent the board to the congregation and others. This person may also be the one who relays board decisions and policies to the congregation. However, like any other individual board person, he doesn't control or tell the senior pastor what to do.[1]

Some people believe that it's better to have a board chairperson, and not the senior pastor, direct the meetings. Here are several reasons.

1. The board chairperson is responsible for setting the board's agenda. If the pastor is experiencing a difficult time at the church, he might be tempted to leave off necessary issues that a board chairperson would include.

2. The pastor might put unnecessary staff issues on the agenda. The board should deal only with board issues.
3. While being the board chairperson isn't a power position, this person will likely have some sway with the board. Thus a pastor's chairing the board could concentrate power in the hands of one person.
4. Separating the positions of board chairperson and senior pastor makes it easier to delineate the functions of the board and those of the pastor and staff.
5. The pastor is an employee of the board and is monitored by them. This could be awkward if the pastor is the board chairperson.
6. If the board chairperson is not the pastor, he is able to provide continuity of leadership when the pastor leaves the church.
7. The board chairperson interprets board policies. This would concentrate much power in the pastor's hands.

Ultimately the decision of whether the pastor should serve as chair depends on the extent to which the board trusts him. In a situation where he's had a lengthy tenure, perhaps the founding pastor, he may serve effectively in the role of board chairperson. But the problem even in this situation is what happens when he does eventually move on or retires and the church is without a pastor for a period of time. And when a new pastor is called, will he have the credibility, knowledge, and experience to chair the board? Allowing the pastor to chair the board may be setting a difficult precedent.

There are several arguments for allowing the senior pastor to function as the board chairperson.

1. The board is intertwined with the pastor and often the staff in the decision-making process. Thus the board's effectiveness is enhanced when its leader is very familiar with the inner workings of the church. In most cases, the pastor and not another chairperson will have this familiarity, except possibly when there's a new pastor or the church is very small.
2. The board and any board chairperson will only be as effective as the pastor wants them to be. The reality is that what the board knows about the church is often dependent on the senior pastor. Board members are part-time, whereas the pastor is full-time and more familiar with the inner workings of the ministry.
3. In some churches there is conflict between the board of leaders and the pastor. In these circumstances, the board and the chairperson can use their position to control or at least neutralize the pastor's

power. This would be more difficult to pull off if the pastor is the board chairperson.

4. If the chairperson doesn't understand the inner workings of the church, this lack of knowledge will diminish the board's effectiveness.

5. An overly zealous or controlling board chairperson could be in a position to manage the church and micromanage the pastor and any staff.

6. The separation of the two leadership positions is easier in theory than in practice. For it to really work, there must be clear agreement, much cooperation, and complementary responsibilities between the board chair and the pastor.

Most would agree that if the senior pastor isn't the board chairperson, he must have a seat at the board table. The obvious reason is that he has the best understanding of the staff and the congregation and should be a full, equal participant in the board's deliberations. The question of who should be board chairperson depends on the individual church. Carter and Lorsch conclude, "Our position about choosing between the two structures is, therefore, pragmatic. Either model can work well, but problems are likely to emerge whatever approach is adopted."[2] The best choice will depend on your situation. Either position can work or be abused. The key is the spiritual maturity of the people involved and the church's circumstances. With a new pastor at the helm, depending on his maturity and leadership ability, it would probably be wise to have a board chairperson. If the pastor is a strong, gifted, experienced leader with good church tenure, he may be the best person to function as the board chairperson.

Board Committees

For help in its ministry, the board may use ministry teams or committees. These teams aren't a part of the board but serve the board in

A committee should never have authority over a board or dictate who is on the governing board.

such tasks as researching an issue or topic, advising, solving problems, monitoring finances, doing a pastoral search, and overseeing senior pastor succession. A committee should never have authority over a board or dictate who is on the governing board. I'm aware of some churches that have a committee on committees that determines who is on the governing board. This takes the power away from the governing board and gives it to a committee, because the latter selects the members of the board. This should never happen!

The board will need to decide whether any of its committees are standing committees, such as the one that does financial monitoring. Others will be temporary, such as the one that aids the board in the selection of a new pastor.

Others

Most boards will have a secretary who may be a member of the board or employed by the board and under its direction. He or she is present to take minutes that are important for legal and historical reasons.[3] This person is ultimately responsible for the integrity of all board documents. Possibly the board will appoint a treasurer, who is familiar with the church's finances. He or she serves to advise the board of how the church is doing financially. In some situations the treasurer may also chair a finance committee.[4] It's impressive when the pastor has the financial expertise to lead these meetings. However, few have this kind of valuable knowledge and most often depend on others who do.

Board Constituents

Board members
Senior pastor
Board chairperson
Board committees
Others

Governing Board Qualifications

Spiritually Mature

As I've said earlier in this work, it's imperative that governing boards be spiritually qualified, because the church's work is spiritual ministry. Since most boards, when they act corporately, have great power to direct the affairs of the church, the members must be spiritually qualified. These qualifications are found in 1 Timothy 3:1–7 and Titus 1:5–9. Other qualifications could be Spirit control and wisdom (Acts 6:3) and the fruit of the Spirit (Gal. 5:22–23).

Reliable and Teachable

Board people should be reliable (trustworthy) and teachable persons (2 Tim. 2:2). A vital ingredient in any leadership equation is trust. A board can't lead people who don't trust them. And the degree to which people trust the board is the degree to which they'll follow their leadership.

This trust is also manifest in teachability. Leaders are learners and therefore should be teachable. When we stop learning, we stop leading, and an indication of whether we're still learning is our teachability. We

---

It's imperative that governing boards be spiritually qualified, because the church's work is spiritual ministry.

---

don't learn from people that we don't trust, so how can we expect people to follow our leadership if we're not teachable? Paul tells Timothy, "And the things you have heard me say . . . entrust to reliable men who will also be qualified to teach others" (2 Tim. 2:2).

In Doctrinal Agreement

Board members must agree with the church's doctrinal statement. The church or current board members must decide, however, whether the doctrinal statement includes the nonessentials of the faith (form of church government, role of women, presence and permanence of sign gifts, divorce and remarriage, when the church meets, and so on) as well as the essentials of the faith (the inspiration and inerrancy of the Bible, the Trinity, the deity and substitutionary atonement of Christ, and the bodily resurrection and return of Christ). See chapter 1 in my book *Doing Church* for more information on the essentials and non-essentials of the faith.[5]

In Alignment with the Church's Values, Mission, Vision, and Strategy

Board members must agree with the church's core values, mission, vision, and strategy (this includes worship style). My friend Gary Blanchard, who is the assistant superintendent of the Illinois District Assemblies of God, once told me, "A discussion on values is key to assimilating new board members. I have found that much of the conflict is oftentimes the result of conflicting values." My experience, along with that of people in the business world, has been the same (see my book *Values-Driven Leadership* for the research that documents this).[6]

Involved Members of the Church

Board members should be members of the church and not just attenders. Membership signals a commitment to the church and alignment with its DNA. They should have been in the church long enough

---

Though they're not to be yes men and should not be expected to rubber-stamp everything, board members do need to be loyal to the senior pastor and his leadership.

---

to have proved themselves (1 Tim. 5:22) through "hands-on" ministry that has involved some kind of leadership. Long enough tenure would be at least two years.

Reasonably Loyal to the Pastor

Though they're not to be yes men and should not be expected to rubber-stamp everything, board members do need to be loyal to the senior pastor and his leadership. If they have a problem with the pastor,

---

Board members shouldn't be preservers of the status quo or tradition but should be open to new ways of doing ministry.

---

they must work with the pastor to seek resolution. If this isn't possible, they should resign from the board.

Respecting Other Board Members

Board members, including the pastor, should care about, genuinely appreciate, and, most important, respect and trust one another (see 1 Tim. 3:2; 2 Tim. 2:2).

Nontraditional

Board members shouldn't be preservers of the status quo or tradition but should be open to new ways of doing ministry. The problem in far too many churches is that board members are in board positions for the very purpose of seeing that things don't change. This attitude kills churches rather than giving them life.

Having Their Spouse's Support

Board members must have the support of their spouse to have an effective ministry. See appendix B for a statement on the role of the board member's spouse.

Board Qualifications

A board member should

Be spiritually qualified

Be reliable and teachable

Be in doctrinal agreement

Be in alignment with the church's DNA

Be an involved member of the church

Be reasonably loyal to the pastor

Respect other board members

Be nontraditional

Have their spouse's support

Recruiting Board Members

It's important to know where members of the congregation are spiritually. Encourage a recruitment culture or mentality. Train the congregation, board, and staff to always be on the lookout for potential, spiritually qualified board members.

Never "fudge" on the qualifications, especially the spiritual qualification. Some churches put an unqualified person on the board, thinking that such an appointment will cause the person to do what is necessary to become spiritually qualified. This never works and the results are usually disastrous. Most often the unqualified person drags down the other members to his or her spiritual level.

Don't be too quick to recruit a person. In addressing the selection of elders, Paul warns in 1 Timothy 5:22 not to be too hasty in the laying on of hands. Give a person time to prove his or her character and competence. Begin by putting the person on an advisory board or perhaps a deacon board, depending on its function.

Since the people on the governing board are some of the church's most spiritually mature people, they, along with the pastor, should identify and seek new people to be on the board. They may want to ask the

---

Train your people to always be on the lookout for potential, spiritually qualified board members.

---

congregation to do this as well and likely will in a congregationally ruled church. However, the pastor and board members should have veto power, based on their knowledge of each nominee.

Selecting Board Members

How will you select board members? The answer depends on the church's polity. In a congregational church, often the board will select those who are qualified and present them to the congregation for final approval. However, in some situations there could be a board nominating committee that chooses the slate that, in turn, goes to the congregation. Thus a congregational rule situation doesn't mean that the congregation has free rein to select anybody and everybody, regardless of their spiritual maturity.

In an elder or board rule congregation, the elders select the new board members. With this method the most spiritually mature people select the church's board leadership. Some elder rule churches will, however, present the selections to the congregation for final approval. In healthy churches, this is merely a rubber stamp.

Monitoring the Board

After leaders are selected for the board, it's important that the board or the congregation monitor their progress. In many churches there is a tendency not to follow up on how a board member is doing. Often, once a person is on the board, he or she is there for life. As would be expected, this produces deadbeat board members. In my experience, few boards remove deadbeat board members, and this, of course, weakens the board.

The solution to this problem is twofold. It involves evaluation and rotation. I'm aware of few churches where the boards involve themselves in any kind of evaluation, either evaluating the board as a whole or its individual members. Evaluation is how boards improve themselves. If the board or its members don't know how they're doing, how can they improve at what they're doing? I strongly recommend that each board member do a self-evaluation and an evaluation of each of the other board members. This could simply be listing the person's strengths and weaknesses as a board leader. Other options are to develop an evaluation form, such as the one below, or to alter the Governing Board Audit in appendix A and use it as your board evaluation.

After the evaluations are completed, the board chairperson or the pastor could review the evaluations with each leader. Should there be any serious problems, the board could put the individual on probation. My experience, however, is that a bad evaluation usually prompts a resignation. In fact I've seen deadbeat members resign when the board merely decided to adopt a performance evaluation process.

Governing Board Evaluation

1. If you have a board chairperson, is his leadership style effective?
2. Do the board chairperson and the pastor work well together?
3. Do the board chairperson and the pastor lead within their respective roles?
4. Does the pastor and/or chairperson encourage board contributions?
5. Is it okay for board members (including the pastor and a chairperson) to disagree among themselves?
6. Do the board members conduct themselves during the meetings in a way that honors the Savior?
7. Do the members support the board's decisions even when one or more disagree with that decision?
8. Do you believe that the board is making a vital contribution to the church and its ministry?
9. Does anyone try to control the board or dominate its meetings?
10. Do any board members ever interfere with the staff's work?

Though few boards review board member performance, many have term limits. Thus, should the board enlist a deadbeat or problematic member, he or she would rotate off the board at the end of the term. The problem with term limits is that you lose good board members when they rotate off. However, even good board leaders need a break from board leadership, and this allows for an injection of new blood that should strengthen board performance. Clearly the advantages of a rotation system outweigh the disadvantages. However, I recommend that each person serve on the board for at least three, preferably four, years before rotating off, because it takes some time to learn the board's business, and if the term is shorter than three years, just about the time a board leader is up to speed, it's time for him or her to rotate off.

What about retirement? Some would ask board people to retire at a certain age, such as seventy. However, it makes no sense to force a leader to retire if he or she is making a valuable contribution to the board.

Questions for Reflection and Discussion

1. Who should serve on a governing board? Is this true in your situation? Why or why not?
2. Do you have a board chairman? Why or why not? Is he the pastor? If so, is this good? Why or why not?
3. What should be the requirements for being on a board? Do you agree with the author's list of qualifications? If not, where do you disagree and why?
4. How should you recruit board members? How do you recruit your board members? Is this good or bad? If it's bad, what do you plan to do about it?
5. How should you select board members? How do you select them? Is this good or bad? If it's bad, what will you do about it?
6. Do you think that there should be term limits for a board? If so, how long should a member serve before rotating off the board?
7. Do you believe that the board's performance should be evaluated (for example, by the congregation or by the board itself)?

6

THE SPIRITUALLY
HEALTHY BOARD
Characteristics of Board Leadership

The importance of a spiritually healthy governing board can't be overstated. It's imperative not only that board members be spiritually healthy, but that they function in a healthy way. A healthy board displays at least four characteristics: They work together as a

The importance of a spiritually healthy governing board can't be overstated. It's imperative not only that board members be spiritually healthy, but that they function in a healthy way.

team; they display courage; they trust and respect one another; they know how to deal with disagreements.

Working as a Team

I'm not aware of any biblical passage that mandates team ministry. However, most leaders in the New Testament worked in teams. This includes the Savior (Mark 6:7) and Paul (Acts 11:22–30; 13:2–3; 15:40). The right people working in a team context often results in a leadership that is characterized by God's wisdom.

Though they work in teams, healthy governing boards have a clearly defined leader. This person is responsible to set the agenda—the direction of the meeting—and keeps the team moving in that direction. While the rest of the team is involved in much that the board does corporately, each board member should step up and contribute from his or her giftedness when dealing with issues that call for a particular expertise (this means that the team members know and understand their divine designs). Thus they know how to contribute individually as well as work together.

It's not unusual for good boards to have differences of opinion. This can be very healthy and assures that the board hears the different sides of an issue when making a decision. Sometimes they may even become emotionally upset with one another. It is important to know how to handle these situations. Strong boards are able to work through them in a spiritually healthy way (Matt. 5:23–24; 18:15–17).

There are basically four team player styles, each corresponding in some manner to the DiSC or Personal Profile System. Each style contributes in different ways to the success of the team. A team member may have one or a combination of styles. And each will have an upside as well as a downside. Following are the four basic team player styles. As you read about each style, identify your unique style. If you read this with your team, identify and discuss your styles.

Challenger. The first style is the Challenger, who has the team player style of the D temperament on the Personal Profile System. This person functions to challenge the team, which involves questioning their goals, methods, and even their ethics. This person is not afraid to disagree with others and to encourage the team to take some risks. He or she is also characterized by candor and openness. The downside of the Challenger is he or she can be insensitive, stubborn, impatient, and inflexible. Also the Challenger will struggle at times to get along with the Contributor.

Motivator. The Motivator has the team player style of the i temperament. This person functions to help the team be optimistic, cooperative, and share ideas. He or she sees the church's vision, is flexible and open to new ideas, and is very good at motivating the others on the team. The Motivator's downside is that he or she can be impulsive, manipulative, and at times obnoxious.

Collaborator. The Collaborator has the team player style of the S temperament. This person functions to help the team collaborate and work well together. He or she is an effective listener, resolves conflicts, and creates an informal, relaxed atmosphere. This person really cares about people. The Collaborator's downside is that he or she can be too conforming, nonconfrontational, and too easygoing.

Contributor. The team player style with the C temperament is the Contributor. This person functions to provide the team with good technical information, data, and quality control and pushes the team to set and observe high performance standards. He or she is attentive to details. The Contributor's downside is that he or she can be fussy, perfectionistic, and stuffy. The Contributor will struggle at times in getting along with the Challenger. They will need to work hard at their relationship so that they can be productive.

Courage

Serving on a church board in the twenty-first century is a leadership intensive enterprise. It's not for the timid or faint of heart (2 Tim.1:7). It requires courage to take necessary risks, stand up for what you believe, address difficult issues, oppose the cynics, accept responsibility, and persevere in difficult times (Josh. 1:6–9; Acts 23:11; 1 Cor. 16:13).

Healthy boards aren't afraid to make the tough decisions. When making such a decision, it's their job to sift through the facts, examine the options, be aware of any biblical directives, and make the best decision

---

Healthy boards aren't afraid to make the tough decisions.

---

possible. In a congregational church, the board does this before taking a decision to the congregation for approval. They also stand behind their decisions, unless it's obvious they made the wrong decision. Later waffling on a good decision, especially when under pressure, is a big mistake that kills board credibility.

Trust and Respect

On an unhealthy board there is a lack of trust, and members are suspicious of one another, leading to disrespect, the sign of an immature, dysfunctional board. When board members respect and care about one another, trust will result, which produces a mature, healthy board.

If a board member wants to be "guardian of the gate" or if board members want to keep an eye on the pastor, little if any trust will be present. These boards are unhealthy and dysfunctional as long as the suspicious attitude prevails.

How can a board develop trust and respect? Here are five ways:

1. Each person must deal with his or her own feelings of mistrust. Determine who on the board you do and don't trust. On a scale of 1 (low) to 10 (high), how would you rate each board person? Do this in a godly, biblical way. Deal with any issues that foment distrust (publicly and privately). These could be past disagreements or other issues. Scripture is very clear that you are to go to the other person and seek reconciliation and forgiveness if necessary—Matthew 5:22–24; 18:15–20.
2. If anyone refuses to deal with issues of mistrust, that person must resign from the board or be asked by the majority to resign.
3. Make a conscientious effort to spend some time together doing things other than board business. (If you don't like this idea, the reason may be that you don't trust or respect the others!) You could go out for coffee after the board meetings or attend various activities together, such as sporting events. It could be said: "The team who plays together stays together."
4. When you enlist new board members, select people who trust others and are without agendas.
5. Work at being open to new, different ideas.

Dealing with Disagreements

As I said above, boards that function well will have disagreements when dealing with issues. This is good because it means that the board is seeing the issue from several sides. In a socially safe environment,

Healthy boards believe: "We can disagree and still be friends."

people will feel free to disagree with one another and won't feel rebuffed or rejected personally because their idea is rejected. Healthy board members learn to separate themselves from their ideas, issues, or viewpoints. Then they don't feel personally attacked when someone disagrees with them, realizing it's the merit of the idea or argument that is being questioned. Everyone on the board knows they can disagree with others and still be friends.

A good way to express disagreement with another's idea or viewpoint on an issue is to ask questions that help the others see why it may not be a good viewpoint or issue to pursue. The Savior used this technique often in his dealing with those with whom he disagreed. Questions make people think rather than react.

Boards would be wise to discuss these matters as a part of the board's training and development process as well as its orientation of new board members.

Characteristics of Healthy Board Leadership

Working together as a team
Displaying courage
Trusting and respecting one another
Dealing well with disagreements

Questions for Reflection and Discussion

1. Do you agree that spiritually healthy boards work together as a team? Why or why not? Is this biblical? Does your board work together as a team? Why or why not?
2. In this chapter did you discover your team player style? What did you discover about yourself? How will you help your team function well? Which of your behaviors or attitudes might keep the team from accomplishing its goals?
3. Why do spiritually healthy boards need to display courage? Is this true of your board? Why or why not?
4. How important is it that board members trust and respect one another? Does your board trust and respect one another? Why or why not? The author gives five ways to develop trust on the board. Which ways would help your board?
5. Does your board deal well with disagreements among themselves? Why or why not? If not, what will you do about it?

THE EFFECTIVE BOARD

Functions of Board Leadership

Those who serve on various boards often operate on the mistaken assumption that all church boards function alike. This is hardly the case as church boards will find themselves leading in different situations with different people. For example, some churches are mired in unhealthy conflict, whereas others are relatively healthy from a spiritual perspective. Some are located in the inner city where they face problems that others located in suburbia only read about in the papers or hear about on CNN. The pastors in some churches may be fresh out of seminary, whereas others are close to retirement. Each presents a different set of circumstances that a board must deal with if it is to have spiritual impact for the Savior.

My board experience, work as a consultant, and research have led me to believe that most boards operate on the basis of uninformed tradition and habit. Somewhere in the past, the typical church formed an initial governance board to serve its needs. And the people who made up that board, drawing on some prior board experience, somehow hammered all this out into what they felt were workable board activities. Over time these became board traditions and habits. Whenever any newcomer joined the board, he or she would be enculturated into these operational traditions. Should the newcomer ask why the board functioned as it did, the answer was, "That's the way we've always done things around here."

Following are some of the more common board functions, based on uninformed board tradition, that I've observed. They range from very hands-off, passive types of boards, serving as rubber stamps, to very hands-on, proactive boards that micromanage. As you read these descriptions, see if any one or a combination of them describes your board situation.

We need to discover how good, spiritually healthy boards function and what they do. In spite of all their diverse circumstances, are there any roles that all share in common? (In this chapter and throughout this

> *We need to discover how good, spiritually healthy boards function and what they do.*

book, I use the terms *functions*, *roles*, and *activities* interchangeably.) This chapter will first look at the problem of how most boards function and then suggest a better way.

The Problem: How Most Boards Function

Rubber Stamps

Some church boards function as rubber stamps. This is the extreme, hands-off, passive board. Of all the ways church boards may function, this incurs the least involvement and time commitment. The board members approve whatever the pastor or some leader, such as a board chairperson or patriarch, wants. It's most characteristic of boards with strong leaders.

I've seen this form in several different ministries. In a church planting situation, the founding pastor will, in time, enlist a governing board. Since he was there first, and all are joining him, he basically tells the board what to do. In growing churches, where the pastor has a long, exemplary tenure, the board is often passive. The pastor has been on the board for a long time and has seen lots of board members come and go. Because of his success and long tenure, the board members trust him implicitly. Thus he often directs the board as to what they will do.

Board members should ask the pastor in this situation, "Are you asking us or are you telling us what to do?"

Guardians of the Gate

Some church boards feel that their job is to keep an eye on the pastor. They function primarily as watchdogs. Initially you might assume this involves pastoral accountability or legitimate monitoring of pastoral performance, but it's more than that. It's about control and preserving the status quo.

These churches and their boards are suspicious of the pastor. Perhaps they've been "burned" by a pastor in their past, so they have a tendency to believe that something is amiss. The former pastor may have led them into extreme debt through a building program only to leave them shortly after it was finished. If the pastor is new, some people are afraid that he's going to change "our church." So they serve on the board primarily to watch over things and keep him in check. My friend Gary Blanchard refers to this as the "union mentality."

The obvious solution to this problem is pastoral credibility that involves trust building. However, this takes time—as much as eight to ten years. Thus pastors who find themselves with such a board must resist the temptation to join the ranks of other pastors who quickly abandon these churches. They must remain committed despite the problems and break the ugly cycle of short-tenured pastors that breed board distrust.

Keepers of the Peace

Though most aren't aware of it, many boards believe that their purpose is to keep everybody happy for the sake of peace and church unity. While this is true in both small and large churches, it's characteristic of many small churches that pride themselves on being one happy family. The board's goal is to keep it that way.

Scripture does encourage unity (Rom. 15:5–6; Eph. 4:1–6) but not at any price. The problem is that some people (the squeaky wheels) realize that to get their way, all they have to do is "squeak"—be unhappy and complain. In case you don't know what I mean by *squeaky wheels*, these people have two characteristics: something is always wrong, and they are very vocal about it. Boards attempt to placate them, which usually means letting them have their way. The result is that a small minority or one or two negative individuals control the church.

The solution is to let the squeaky wheels squeak. Don't oil them, regardless of how loud they get. You should give them a hearing (occasionally they're right), but the board's job is not to do what the problem people prefer. The board must do what God prefers as he gives direction to the board.

Representative Democracies

As we move closer to the other extreme of typical boards (more hands-on), we discover that many boards believe their job is to represent the various groups (often factions) within the church, to see that their interests are protected at the board level. They view their function or role as involved representatives in a church that they believe is a representative democracy—at least that's been their tradition. But leaders are called to lead not represent various church groups, especially factions. Factions characterize spiritually unhealthy churches (1 Cor. 1:10–17; 3:1–9). The idea behind a representative democracy is that all opinions are equal, but in reality they aren't. Some are better than others, and informed opinions are better than uninformed opinions.

Mundane Micromanagers

In small churches in particular, boards tend to micromanage the church. It is the most proactive, hands-on, time-consuming board approach. There are several reasons why church boards micromanage. One is high pastoral turnover. Pastoral tenure early in the twenty-first century averages around three to four years. The board has the responsibility to carry on the church's business, especially when there is no pastor.

A hands-on board may also be attempting to assist a pastor who is very busy and may be bivocational. In some cases, the church hires a pastor to do the work of the ministry (preach, pray, do weddings and funerals, and perform other similar functions) while the board runs the church (this is a reversal of the biblical emphasis, as in Eph. 4:11–13).

The problem is that micromanaging the church guarantees that it will remain small and ineffective.

Some boards micromanage because there is a power play taking place. The pastor wants the power to lead, but the board is resisting it.

The problem is that micromanaging the church guarantees that it will remain small and ineffective. In many cases it reveals a lack of trust in the staff, creates leadership and operational bottlenecks, and stifles creativity. It also guarantees that the board will not deal with the more important issues, such as church direction, strategy, and doctrine.

The Solution: How Boards Should Function

It is wise for every board to pause and examine what they're doing or not doing. They must ask, What should our role be as a board that has a passion to serve Christ? I believe that most boards are to be involved with some mix of at least four primary functions as leaders of leaders: praying, monitoring, deciding, and advising.

Before we look at these, I must briefly address the two external constraints that affect boards in how they approach these four roles. One is the Scriptures. The board's functions must align with the clear teaching of Scripture. And where Scripture is prescriptive, we must be prescriptive. But where Scripture is silent, we have much freedom as long as that freedom doesn't conflict with Scripture in any way (see this discussion in chapter 3).

The other form of constraint is legal. The board must operate within the law (which also agrees with Scripture—Rom. 13:1–6). Churches need to be aware of any state or local laws that might affect how they operate, especially those regarding a church's incorporation within its state of residence. In North America as well as other countries, the legal framework allows the church much freedom within which to function.

In this discussion, we must also keep in mind that most boards are made up of part-time people. This means that they have limited time for board work (four to six hours a month), limited expertise, and are physically removed from the ministry site. There is no way that a board, even in the smallest church, can control every action, circumstance, or decision. Consequently, they must take these realities into consideration when deciding what they will do and how they will do it, or the board will never accomplish its goals and be most frustrated much of the time.

The solution to micromanaging is delegate, delegate, delegate! Leave any micromanaging to the staff, those on the front lines of ministry who know best what to do. Let the staff lead and handle the day-to-day operations of the church. In *The Unity Factor*, Pastor Larry Osborne supplies us with three excellent, well thought through reasons for this.[1]

The first is *time*. The staff not laypersons work with the entire church on a day-to-day (eight to ten hours plus) basis. They know the church inside and out. They face the problems and opportunities of the church full-time. And over time, they develop a feel for and are able to read these matters.

Changes happen quickly; many decisions can't wait until a board meets. They need to be made on the spot. The board needs to delegate on-the-spot authority to pastors to make these decisions, and pastors must entrust the same to people on their staff.

Some laypersons may be very good at leading corporate organizations, but they do it on a full-time basis on location. They would not attempt to do it part-time off location. The same principle applies to the church, which is so much more important than any corporate organization. Management must be done by full-time staff.

The second reason that staff should do the managing is their *training*. Most staff leaders have more training for church ministry than lay leaders. (However, some have only been trained to teach and preach with little preparation for leadership. It's imperative that these staff people be retooled.) Most competent staff involve themselves in continuing education regarding church ministry and leadership. And most have a network of peers with whom they spend time, drawing from their experiences and knowledge.

Staff members are *close to their ministries* and know and understand them much better than does the board. Since they carry out ministry and are affected by a decision about their ministry, they should make the decisions or have much input into them. Wise boards either let the staff make those decisions or heavily involve the staff in them. The collective wisdom of individual ignorance can be devastating to team morale!

Four Universal Board Functions

Let's now examine the four universal board functions.

PRAYING

Prayer is essential, not optional, for every board. As Howard Hendricks of Dallas Seminary would say, "It's their spiritual breathing apparatus." Paul exhorts the believers at Thessalonica to pray constantly. If the "troops" are to pray constantly, the leaders need to set the example. The board must pray for the congregation, the pastoral staff, and themselves.

There is precedent for elders praying on behalf of those in their congregation. Twice James mentions prayer in James 5:13, and in verses 14–15 he encourages the people to whom he's writing to call on their elders or leaders to pray for them, specifically when they are sick.

A board must also pray for the staff. A significant number of pastors and members of their staff have left the ministry due to moral indiscretion. I wonder how many of these pastors and staff persons had boards who backed them up with constant, prevailing prayer. I suspect that the answer is very few.

The board that prays together and for one another usually works well and stays together. Fervent, soul-wrenching prayer has a way of breaking down any walls that separate people and builds spiritual and emotional

---

Prayer is essential, not optional, for every board.

---

bonds between them. The board might consider not only praying at its meetings but getting together at other times in pairs or groups to pray. This could be done as they meet for breakfast, lunch, or at other times, praying for the staff and congregation and the implementation of its values, mission, vision, and strategy.

MONITORING

Monitoring is another word for overseeing. Apparently the elders in the New Testament served as overseers. In Acts 20:28 Paul exhorts the elders of the city church of Ephesus to "keep watch over yourselves and all the flock." That's congregational oversight. In 1 Timothy 3:2 Paul uses the term *overseer* again when he introduces the various qualifications for those who desire to be elders.

I use the term *monitoring* instead of *overseeing* only because it's better understood in today's early twenty-first-century culture and means the same thing. Church boards can lead by monitoring the church and the senior pastor, focusing specifically on the church's spiritual condition, theology, and ministry direction.

The Church's Spiritual Condition

Twenty-first-century churches face the dilemma of a pastoral revolving door, with the average tenure of a pastor being three to four years in a church. When a pastor leaves, the church's leadership falls squarely on the shoulders of the church's governing board. It is their responsibility to monitor the church's spiritual condition during the pastoral search, which may last several years. While the church has a pastor, the board must be monitoring the spiritual condition of the church along with its pastor. Then, when the pastor leaves, they are already aware of how the church is doing spiritually.

In addition, some pastors, in their passion for some aspect of their ministry such as preaching or pastoral care, might be prone to let the spiritual state of the congregation slip. Again, the board, while monitoring the pastor's ministry, is responsible to keep their finger on the church's spiritual pulse as well.

Thus the board should regularly check the spiritual vital signs of the church, whether with or without a pastor. Spiritually healthy churches have a vital spirituality, but in every church the board must consistently

---

The board must consistently ask, How are we doing spiritually?

---

ask, How are we doing spiritually? Are we a vital, Christ-honoring body? Or are we dragging spiritually, and if so, why?

The Church's Essential Biblical Doctrine

The board must be sure that the church's theology agrees with the essential doctrines of the Bible. That's the positive side. The negative side is to protect the church from false teaching or bad doctrine. This is the particular point that Paul is making with the Ephesian pastors in Acts 20:28–31. The New Testament frequently warns us against false teachers and their teaching. Apparently it was a huge problem at that time, just as it is today.

I've used the adjective *essential* for a reason. I divide a church's beliefs into the essentials and the nonessentials. The former refers to those propositional truths that not only are clearly taught in the Bible but are also necessary to hold if one is to be considered orthodox.[2] These include the inspiration of the Bible, the Trinity, the deity and substitutionary atonement of Christ, and the other orthodox beliefs. The nonessentials are those beliefs about church government, the mode of baptism, the role of women in the church, the presence or absence of the sign gifts, and other similar views. Regardless, the board must take responsibility to discern what is essential and nonessential for its church, articulate this in a doctrinal statement, and protect the church from those who would teach otherwise. I have difficulty understanding churches that pride themselves in not having a doctrinal statement. A doctrinal statement assures that the body knows what they believe.

"Those who would teach otherwise" include other board members, the pastor in particular, any staff, the church's teachers, and any members who espouse a different theology. I say "the pastor in particular" because the only ones who have the authority and power to protect the congregation from a doctrinally aberrant pastor is the board. The pastor is responsible for recruiting a staff that is doctrinally sound, and all should keep an ear attuned to the congregation for any questionable teaching.

All of this assumes that boards have a working knowledge of the Bible and theology. The truth is that most don't. And those that don't will have a difficult time monitoring the church's beliefs. Thus it is incumbent on them to gain this knowledge. I'm responsible for elder leadership development on the board that I serve with at my church. To address this issue, we spent a number of meetings reading through and discussing Charles Ryrie's *A Survey of Bible Doctrine*.[3] This is a survey of systematic theology written at the level of the person who sits in the pew. The entire board agreed that our study served to sharpen and shape our knowledge in this vital area. I believe that it would help you as well.

The Church's Biblical Ministry Direction

The board is to hold the church to its biblical ministry direction. Here I'm using the term *church* corporately. I'm including the congregation, staff, and the board itself. The term *ministry direction* includes both the church's mission and vision. Every church's biblical mission and vision are based on the Great Commission (Matt. 28:19–20). The church's mission is a short, memorable statement of the Great Commission. An example is "The church's mission is to make and mature believers at home and abroad." The church's vision is what that will

---

Every church's biblical mission and vision are based on the Great Commission.

---

look like when the church begins to make and mature believers in its ministry community.

The board along with the pastor is to protect and cast the church's mission and vision. They must protect the mission and vision from being diluted by all the other issues in general and problems in particular that surface to distract churches from what they're supposed to be doing. The problem for churches is that they tend to get lost in ministry minutiae and thus are sidetracked from their mission. The board is to hold the church to its biblical course and not allow it to become a niche church, pursuing some aspect of the commission and not the commission itself. As Stephen Covey would say, for the board, the main thing is to keep the main thing the main thing.

The board can help cast the vision by regularly reminding themselves, the pastor, the staff, and the congregation of their mission as a church and how that translates into the church's vision. They could do this through a regular monthly statistical update on the church's evangelism efforts, weekly worship attendance, giving, and any other vital signs that show how the ministry is progressing in terms of making and maturing believers.

The Pastor's Leadership

The board is responsible for overseeing the pastor's leadership and ministry, and he is responsible to the board for that ministry. To say that he's only responsible to God and no one else is irresponsible. The new paradigm approach found in this book strikes a balance of power between the pastor and the governing board, as opposed to one entity having all the power. (See appendix J for a discussion of power.) Here the emphasis is on the board's relationship to the pastor.

The board should informally monitor the pastor's performance throughout the ministry year, using the policies that it has articulated for his role. It could formally evaluate the pastor at least once a year. The board is responsible for addressing any questionable ideas or behavior. In this way the board will also serve to provide the pastor with necessary accountability. Perhaps a member or two of the board will

The idea here isn't to control him or keep him in check but to care for and minister to his soul.

assume the responsibility for meeting with the pastor monthly for accountability purposes—to ask the hard questions about his personal life. The idea here isn't to control him or keep him in check but to care for and minister to his soul.

DECIDING

I believe that most board members would agree that, more than anything else, the board has to make lots of decisions, especially "sink the ship" kinds of decisions, such as the selection or dismissal of a pastor, a relocation to another facility, or a major capital funds project. The board will spend significant time on these decisions. This was common with various gatherings in the New Testament—though they weren't necessarily boards, as I'm using them in this work. For example, the Twelve made a critical decision in the life of the Jerusalem church (Acts 6:2–4) and then gathered the disciples to announce that decision. And much the same took place at the Jerusalem Council in Acts 15.

Thus the board must decide how it will make decisions. What are the guidelines, if any, for its decision making? The answer to this and other board issues is to draft church governance policies. Then most of its decisions should be made on the basis of the policies approach. I define policies as the standard decisions in answer to important, often repetitive questions or problems. The board should regularly make and review church policies in three areas: the board's functions, the senior pastor's functions, and the relationship of the board to the senior pastor. It may also address policies that affect its personnel (personnel policies) and the congregation (congregational policies). We'll pursue further the policy making approach in the next chapter.

ADVISING

Wise pastors look to their boards for advice. And wise boards give it. There is no perfect pastor. Though they weren't necessarily pastors of a church, Timothy and Titus were the constant recipients of Paul's advice. All pastors make mistakes—some huge, some small, and lots ranging somewhere in between. Therefore, if the board is made up of godly, spiritual people, it's incumbent on the pastor to seek and savor their advice before making decisions affecting the church. Getting another perspective on a situation helps to spot and head off biased or uninformed decisions.

An important point to keep in mind is that a board's advice is different from its decision making. It's not imperative that the pastor or staff follow the board's advice; they have a choice. However, when the leadership board makes a decision, it is final, and the pastor and staff are expected to concur with it and follow through on it.

The Governing Board's Primary Responsibilities

Praying

Monitoring

Deciding

Advising

One word of caution when discussing and working your way through these leadership functions or roles. Make sure that you communicate clearly. Many of us have different meanings for the same words. So be careful to define your terms. Be clear when describing the board's roles of *monitoring*, *deciding*, and *advising*. Using illustrations can help immensely.

Four Occasional Board Functions

In addition to the four primary board functions, the board will likely exercise some additional responsibilities. However, they will have to do these only rarely, if ever. Thus I refer to them as occasional functions. I give four of them below.

SELECTING THE SENIOR PASTOR

When a pastor leaves a church's ministry, someone must take responsibility for searching for and selecting a new pastor. Usually the governing board plays a role in this. The board's involvement in the selection of a pastor will depend to some extent on the church's polity. If the church is under congregational rule, the congregation will select the next pastor. If it's board-driven, the board will have the option of selecting the new pastor.

Regardless of polity, the board can and should exert much influence on the process. For example, in a congregationally ruled church, often it's the pulpit committee that determines which candidate goes to the congregation for a final vote. However, the board, as spiritually mature leaders in the church, could and should be involved in some way in making these determinations. The board could serve as the pulpit committee, appoint some of its members to the committee, or monitor the actions of the committee.

This doesn't mean, however, that the board chooses other pastoral staff. This is the sole responsibility of the senior pastor not the board. If the church is without a senior pastor and in need of staff persons, the board must wait until the church has a pastor and let him choose other staff persons. However, a wise senior pastor will likely involve the board in this process, especially in larger churches where staff persons serve at an executive level.

In addition to its involvement in selecting the senior pastor, I believe that the board is responsible for addressing the issue of pastoral succession. Once a senior pastor reaches sixty, if not earlier, the board along with the pastor should begin to discuss his succession, regardless of

The board is responsible for addressing the issue of pastoral succession.

when he expects to retire. The pastor should make the board aware of his plans for future ministry, retirement, and a potential successor. For example, will the church look to someone already on staff or will it bring someone in from the outside? Will the current pastor groom this person for the position or will the board wait until the pastor actually retires? And will the board recommend that the retiring pastor stay in the church or would it be best for the new pastor if he moved on to another church? The latter may seem harsh; however, there are numerous horror stories of retiring pastors who stayed in the church only to become an unintentional, and sometimes intentional, source of problems for the new pastor.

ARBITRATING DISPUTES

Since there is no perfect church and no perfect pastor, there will be times when differences over any number of issues will arise. Every church should have in place a grievance process to deal with people and their issues. People, such as church staff, church members, and even those outside the church, may have problems with the church. If a person's problem is with the senior pastor, it's biblically imperative that he or she go first to the pastor and attempt to resolve any issues at that level. Matthew 18:15 is very clear: "If your brother sins against you, go and show him his fault, just between the two of you. If he listens to you, you have won your brother over."

My experience is that getting the disputing parties together will usually settle the problem. The reason is that most of us could do a much better job communicating, and thus most of our problems are based on miscommunication. When disputing parties get together, they communicate better and often resolve their issues privately. However, if the issue with a senior pastor isn't resolved at this level, then it could go to the board whose corporate decision would be final.

PROTECTING THE PASTOR

In far too many ministries there exist people whom I call church bullies. These are people who for various reasons don't like the senior pastor and do everything within their power to undermine him and/or his ministry, hoping that he'll leave the church. I know of one situation where two such bullies didn't get their way in the selection of a new pastor. Thus they committed themselves to doing everything possible to get rid of the selected pastor. Unfortunately no one did anything to deal with the situation, and eventually the church bullies won (but the church lost), and the new pastor left.

Clearly the governing board is responsible for dealing with such a situation. As the opposition set in, the board should have gone to each man individually, informing him that they knew what he was doing, and if he didn't stop, the board would commence church discipline against him, according to Matthew 18:15–19. Another option would be to skip the warning and simply commence the discipline process. This would allow the board to deal with any gossip or other sin that bullies might spread prior to being warned.

It's imperative that boards not stand by and watch this kind of thing take place. It puts the pastor in the difficult position of having to defend himself. And if he leaves, it encourages the bullies to engage in a repeat

---

When boards begin to deal with church bullies, the word gets out and the bullies go elsewhere or repent.

---

performance. However, when boards begin to deal with church bullies, the word gets out and the bullies go elsewhere or repent.

ORDAINING AND LICENSING

On behalf of the church, the board will ordain those whom it feels God is leading into full-time ministry, such as a senior pastor or leadership staff person in a church. In some instances it may be people who are teaching in a seminary or Bible school as well as those who are itinerant Bible teachers and missionaries.

Since these people must be spiritually qualified, the board needs to have observed them and their ministries and know them well enough to affirm that they meet the qualifications, as outlined in 1 Timothy 3:1–7 and Titus 1:6–9. The applicant for ordination must demonstrate knowledge of the Bible and theology. He or she may or may not have had formal theological preparation.

The board will license those whom it feels God is leading into church or parachurch ministry on a full- or part-time basis. Licensure is for those who are spiritually qualified but may not have had any theological preparation. They're usually not ministering in a lead pastoral role but may be specialists in a church or parachurch ministry.

The Governing Board's Occasional Responsibilities

Selecting the senior pastor
Arbitrating disputes
Protecting the senior pastor
Ordaining and licensing qualified people for ministry

Other Factors Affecting Board Function

Earlier in this chapter when describing the board's roles or functions, I described them as *some mix of at least four primary functions:*

praying, monitoring, deciding, and advising. I say *some mix*, because boards can't emphasize all four roles equally. A particular board will focus on certain roles in its leadership context and will have less focus on others, depending on the church's needs and circumstances. In this final section, I want to address the mix component of these functions. At least two factors affect how a board will think about the mix of these components. The first is the church's ministry circumstances, which include the church's ministry performance and the board's relationship with the pastor. The second is the board members' personal qualities, which they bring to the equation as leaders of leaders.

The Church's Ministry Circumstances

MINISTRY PERFORMANCE

A church's ministry performance will address how involved the board will be in the ministry and which functions it will stress. For example, if the church is doing well and accomplishing its mission—it is reaching lost people and maturing its saved people—the board may sit back and play more of a monitoring role. However, it must tirelessly guard against complacency. The primary enemy of biblically

---

The primary enemy of biblically based, spiritually healthy churches is complacency.

---

based, spiritually healthy churches is complacency. So, in these good situations, the board should be on a constant hunt for self-satisfaction in the ministry ranks.

If, on the other hand, the church is in trouble or going through a time of momentous change, either within the church itself or in the community where it is located, the board may need to be more engaged in more roles (without micromanaging). Every church moves through a life cycle. It's born or planted and initially grows. Yet over time it tends to focus inward, which sends it into a plateau and eventual decline. When the church is plateaued or in decline, it has reached a critical point in its life and the board must then take notice and become more involved. The same holds true in momentous change, such as when there is lots of movement of people into or out of the community. Boards that assume the ostrich position and ignore such situations do the church grave harm.

Another factor affecting the church's ministry performance is the board's relationship with the senior pastor. Most leadership boards understand that they must work effectively with the senior pastor if the ministry is to accomplish its mission and vision—make disciples (Matt. 28:19–20). However, rarely do leadership boards address the best ways to lead and minister with their pastors. Instead, the relationship tends to evolve over a period of time. The problem with this is that an unclear relationship leads to misunderstanding and conflicts, all of which result in a breakdown of trust. And leadership can't take place in a context of mistrust.

When there's an unclear relationship and the pastor is new to the church, the board will often find itself tightening the reins, trying to retain control. The board thinks the new pastor needs to prove himself before they let him lead. In time their relationship will likely change if the pastor leads well and gains the respect and confidence of the board. They will become less proactive and will allow him more room to lead. Again, the problem is that not many pastors are staying around long enough to build this kind of confidence.

The most problematic relationship develops when the board discovers that the pastor isn't a leader or has a view of how he is to function in ministry that is different from that of the board. The pastor may be an excellent Bible teacher or preacher but doesn't have a clue about how to lead the board, much less the church. Or what he learned in seminary about how to lead a church (the "scholar behind the closed door" ministry model) isn't what the church is used to or wants in a pastor. The result is that the board has little if any confidence in the

Whatever the situation, the only way to deal with the board-pastor relationship is to explicitly discuss both roles so that all have a shared understanding.

pastor and will likely take over the leadership of the church, which has disastrous consequences.

Whatever the situation, the only way to deal with the board-pastor relationship is to explicitly discuss both roles so that all have a shared understanding. This discussion must take place with potential pastors before they're offered a position in the church and must be clarified with established pastors so that all will have a common understanding. The established pastor may not agree entirely with the board's role, but at least he'll have a clear idea of where the board stands on the matter. In the same way, the board will understand the pastor's position and feelings about the role of the board.

The Board Members' Personal Qualities

A most important factor affecting the board's function is the personal qualities of each member. It's important to know what personal qualities characterize a good board person, so that these people can be asked to serve on the board. It's imperative that the board discuss and agree on the fundamental personal qualities that make up a good board person. An effective board member will have some or all of the qualities listed in chapter 5.

GODLY CHARACTER

Board members are leaders of leaders. Therefore, they must set a spiritual example for all other leaders and people in the church. Paul's words to Timothy ring clear for all leaders at the board level when he writes, "Train yourself to be godly. For physical training is of some value, but godliness has value for all things, holding promise for both the present life and the life to come" (1 Tim. 4:7–8). Consequently, they should meet the qualifications set forth in such passages as 1 Timothy 3:1–13; Titus 1:5–9; and 1 Peter 5:1–3 (see appendices G and H for a character audit). This disqualifies "good old boys"—those who don't meet the spiritual qualifications but have been in the church for a long time.

DOCTRINAL AGREEMENT

Leaders of leaders must know and agree with the church's doctrinal statement. Paul's multiple exhortations throughout Scripture to be on the lookout for false doctrine and false teachers imply that the first-century churches knew what was sound doctrine and that their churches had some kind of doctrinal statements (see for example 1 Tim. 3:16).

INTERPERSONAL SKILLS

Board leaders must be able to get along with one another as well as the pastor, the staff, and the rest of the congregation. This requires good people skills. Following are a few questions to ask. Do they relate well with people? How well do they work with groups? Are they team players? Are they good listeners as well as talkers (James 1:19)?

INTELLECTUAL CAPACITY

Board leaders must be good thinkers. What they do is often very cerebral. They should understand the church and how it works. They have to think well in the functions of deciding and advising and need to be able to think their way through the church's business. And knowledge of boards in general and the church's board in particular is vital. The new board member will not know all that's needed to lead well. And much of this knowledge will come from involvement—leaders learn as they serve.

EMOTIONAL CAPACITY

Spiritually healthy boards are made up of emotionally healthy people. Perhaps an illustration is worth the proverbial thousand words. Would you rather work along with and be led by Billy Graham or Adolph Hitler? The point is that one is characterized by good emotional capacity—love, joy, peace, and so on; whereas, the other operates through fear, anger, intimidation, and so on. While the latter doesn't sound very Christian, I'm aware of boards that function this way and are led by pastors or board chairmen who attempt to lead by creating an environment of fear and intimidation.

COMMITMENT TO THE CHURCH

Those who would lead the church must be committed to the church—who it is (its DNA) and what it does (some would call this its philosophy of ministry). They must agree and align with its core values. This assumes that they as well as the church know what they are. They must be reasonably passionate about the church's mission and vision—"make disciples." They must also agree with the strategy that includes such issues as who they hope to reach and how they plan to reach these people. This includes the church's worship style. This quality shouldn't be a major problem as the board will be involved in determining these matters. This kind of commitment would also involve one's time. Potential board persons are wise to ask, What is the time commitment and am I willing to enthusiastically make this time commitment to my church to serve on this leadership board?

LOYALTY TO THE PASTOR

Loyalty to the pastor means that one is willing to work with and support the senior or only pastor. He or she believes that the pastor is God's person to lead the church. This isn't a blind loyalty. It's a kind of loyalty that includes challenging as well as supporting this person. Those who struggle with authority figures, have a gripe with the pastor, believe that they've been wronged by him, or question his leadership "need not apply." And it's not that these are necessarily bad people. The problem is that these other issues would cloud their judgment and thus affect their abilities to work with a board led by someone with whom they struggle at a spiritual and leadership level.

Church leadership boards that perform poorly most often have members that are deficient in one or several of these personal qualities. And churches that are struggling often have these deficient people sitting on their boards. Churches must resist the temptation to put just anyone or good old boys on their boards. Instead, they would show wisdom by selecting people with these qualities or waiting for God to bring them along.

Questions for Reflection and Discussion

1. The author lists a number of functions that he believes are not appropriate for church boards. In general do you agree? Do you disagree with any of them? If so, which and why? Do any of these practices characterize your church? If so, which ones?
2. The author gives three reasons why he believes that a board shouldn't micromanage the church. What are they? Do you agree with them? Do you disagree on any? If so, why?
3. The author lists four primary and four occasional board functions. Which do you agree with? Which do you not agree with? Why? How many of these are functions of your board? How many should be functions of your board?

8

THE POLICIES APPROACH TO GOVERNANCE

Operations of Board Leadership

The effective board operates by using a policies governance model. Leading or governing by policy is a whole new, revolutionary approach to developing governing boards that lead with excellence. The premise of the policies governance model is that good governance

---

Leading or governing by policy is a whole new, revolutionary approach to developing governing boards that lead with excellence.

---

boards will lead and operate using policies arrived at by the consensus of their members.

John Carver developed this model for use in the not-for-profit sector in 1990. I recommend his two books: *Boards That Make a Difference* and

Reinventing Your Board, as well as the *Carver Guide Series on Effective Board Leadership*, a series of pamphlets on board governance, published by Jossey-Bass. Much but by no means all of what is said here and in the next few chapters on the policies approach reflects Carver's thinking. Those who are familiar with Carver's material will note certain fundamental disagreements, however.

What Is the Policies Approach?

The policies approach argues that boards exist to do a number of things, one of which is to lead by policies. It isn't simply a new name for the same old board work; it's a radically new approach to functioning as a leadership board. Therefore, you can't implement it by simply changing the names of what you're doing or tweaking the old process (making only a few changes here or there).

One of the board's main functions according to chapter 7 is decision making. Key to good decision making is wise decision making. And the way that boards make wise decisions is through the use of clear, consistent policies based on biblical directives. *I define policies as the beliefs and values that consistently guide or direct how a church or parachurch*

It isn't simply a new name for the same old board work; it's a radically new approach to functioning as a board.

---

governing board makes its decisions. These are standard decisions that answer questions or problems that are important and often repetitive. Thus the policies are vital guidelines for decision making.

It's imperative that the board base its policies on the Scriptures. However, my board experience has shown that Scripture doesn't address many of the areas where policies are needed to lead the church. If it did, the Bible would likely be a huge, unwieldy book. Where Scripture doesn't address an issue, the board should proceed to make policy; only it must be careful to develop policies that don't violate in any way the clear teaching of Scripture.

Decisions based on policies affect four primary areas:

1. *The board's job or function.* The board's governance policies will define its job and thus its expectations of itself.

2. *The senior pastor's job and his expectations as well as limits.* These policies define the senior pastor's ministry responsibilities and the board's expectations of him.

3. *The relationship between the board and the senior pastor.* These policies define the board–senior pastor relationship, identifying what the board delegates to the pastor.

4. *The church's ministry ends or its mission.* These policies are the board's expectations about the outcome of the church's mission and vision in the lives of the people to whom it ministers. However, if a church has already developed its mission statement along with a strategic planning process, it may or may not want to include that mission under its policies.

These four policy areas aren't the only policies that affect the church. Most churches should have policies that cover at least two other areas. One is the church's personnel. Personnel policies are those that affect employment, wages and salary, employee benefits, employee conduct, and other areas related to the church's full- and part-time personnel. The church should also have policies concerning the congregation. Congregational policies address such matters as church membership, child care, weddings, funerals, benevolence, counseling, provisions for the handicapped, medical emergencies, use of facilities and properties, a grievance process, discipline, and other topics related to and focusing on congregational life. The governing board may and often does address

Policies function much like the boundaries, end lines, and goal lines of a football field.

personnel and congregational policies, if only to grant its approval. In some cases, the staff will develop and handle them (especially congregational policies) without board involvement. Each church will decide what works best for it. In this book I will focus on the first four policy areas not the latter two.

The policies dealing with the board, senior pastor, and board–senior pastor relationship function much like the boundaries, end lines, and goal lines of a football field. They define where the board (coach) and the senior pastor (quarterback) operate and determine in which areas they should make decisions and in which they should not (where they can score a touchdown and where they are out of bounds). The policy governance approach requires that the board articulate and record its policies in a notebook or an official document and use them to consistently guide itself in the many decisions it has to make as it serves the ministry.

Four Areas of Policy Development

Board function

Senior pastor function

Board–senior pastor relationship

Church's mission (ministry ends)

The Advantage of Using a Policies Approach

Following are eleven advantages that a policies approach contributes to good board governance.

1. Unlike the church's staff, a governing board is limited in terms of the time that it has available to serve, its ministry expertise, and its off-site presence. However, the policies approach allows it to deal with the most fundamental, lasting elements of the church instead of tons of trivia. Thus the board focuses on the big picture, the major issues.

2. Focusing on the most fundamental, enduring issues of the church enables the board to have the greatest impact in the least amount of time.

3. A policies approach minimizes board interference with the senior pastor. The board lets the senior pastor be the senior pastor and do what he, not they, has the expertise to do. With policies in hand, he knows the board's expectations, the lines of authority, and generally what he can and can't do.

4. The policies approach minimizes board interference with the staff and their responsibilities. The board makes policies that set boundaries and expectations for the staff. Then the staff is free to work within those boundaries under the leadership of the senior pastor.

5. A policies approach enables past, present, and future boards to make consistent rather than arbitrary decisions that affect the ministry. This is because, over the years, they all use essentially the same written policies to make those decisions.

6. Policy use eliminates ministry minutiae at board meetings. Policies are broad guidelines that cover and often predecide a number

of smaller issues. Rather than having to make separate decisions as issues come to the board's attention (event decision making), policies already in place may cover many or most of them, which means a decision has already been made.

7. Using policies makes for shorter meetings with shortened agendas, because often a policy is already in place that decides the issue. Thus board members spend less time discussing and debating issues.

8. A policies perspective encourages good attendance of as well as a good spirit at board meetings because board members feel that they're accomplishing something worth their time and effort.

9. A policies approach enables the board to establish clear lines of authority between itself and the senior pastor and staff.

10. Having policies results in more trust between the board and the senior pastor because both know what is expected of the other.

11. Clear policies prevent an individual or small group of people from controlling the decision-making processes that affect the church. They must follow or operate by established policies not by what they personally want to do or see happen in a particular situation.

The Advantages of Using a Policy Approach

It deals with essential, fundamental church matters.
It allows for the most impact in the least amount of time.
It minimizes board interference with the senior pastor.
It minimizes board interference with the staff.
It allows for consistent decisions through the years.
It eliminates focusing on ministry minutiae at meetings.
It makes for shorter board meetings.
It encourages good attendance at board meetings.
It establishes clear lines of authority between the board and the pastor.
It engenders trust between the board and pastor.
It prevents an individual or group from controlling the decision-making process.

How the Policies Approach Works

Ministry Means and Ends

According to Carver's policy governance model, the board must address four categories of organizational decisions for which it is accountable. For the church these would be policies affecting the board, policies affecting the pastor, policies affecting the board-pastor relationship, and policies affecting ministry direction. The first three deal with ministry means and the last with ministry ends, which are policies that affect decisions involving the ministry's direction or mission and vision.

Categories of Organizational Decisions

Ministry Means
Policies affecting the board
Policies affecting the pastor
Policies affecting the board-pastor relationship

Ministry Ends
Policies affecting ministry direction (mission and vision)

It's possible that, contrary to Carver's advice, the board may want to address only the three categories that fall under ministry means—policies affecting the board, policies affecting the pastor, and policies affecting the board-pastor relationship. This would work when the board has already very clearly addressed the church's direction and regularly monitors it. This is what I recommend in my books *Advanced Strategic Planning* and *Ministry Nuts and Bolts*.[1]

Permitting and Prohibiting Certain Functions

The board may set policies that both permit and prohibit what the board or the senior pastor can do. Leaders need to know what they can do and what they're supposed to accomplish. The policies provide the board's expectations of achievement, and the pastor needs to make sure that he accomplishes these expectations if he is to fulfill the responsibilities of his job. Carver would not agree with this. He would argue that

The board may set policies that both permit and prohibit what the board itself or the senior pastor can do.

the next paragraph articulating what leaders can't do better describes the point leader's role in the organization than this paragraph does.[2] I'll address this in the next chapter.

Leaders need to know what they can't do. Policies provide pastors with limitations, so they know what is out of bounds. Though this sounds negative, it is extremely freeing, because it means that the senior pastor can use any means that the board hasn't prohibited and he doesn't have to spend precious time waiting for the board to meet monthly or bimonthly to approve his plans. With this approach, boards and pastors no longer have to guess at expectations.

Interpreting Board Policies

The board establishes policies at various levels that allow it to delegate comfortably to the senior pastor, who then must interpret what he can do within the confines of that level. Some policies are broad, leaving lots of room for interpretation. They are considered level 1 or possibly level 2 policies. Other policies—levels 3 and 4—are narrow, leaving less room for interpretation. These will be discussed further in chapter 9.

The board begins with the most general policies that allow the least board control and the broadest interpretation by the senior pastor and the board chairperson, if there is one. However, the more the board wants to have a say about or control over an issue, the more it systematically narrows the policies, moving from the broadest (levels 1 or 2) to more narrow levels (such as levels 3 or 4).

The board will move from level to level (from higher to lower levels) until it reaches the level where it's comfortable allowing the senior pastor to make any reasonable interpretation of the policy that is possible at that level.[3] If this isn't entirely clear, I will walk you through it, using a specific example in the next chapter.

Board Decisions

I argue that a governing board should use consensus not compromise to develop and establish its policies. Many boards make decisions through compromise. With compromise, everyone gives a little to reach

I argue that a governing board should use consensus not compromise to develop and establish its policies.

a decision. However, that decision is often insipid, and few are happy with the final result.

A much better approach is to operate by consensus. A board must define what it means by consensus. It can range from all must agree (unanimity) to a simple majority where the number of votes required to win is one. The latter is preferable. However, if the board achieves a simple majority, such a close vote may, but does not necessarily, signal a need for further discussion, prayer, and delaying the final decision until the next board meeting. This will depend on how much the board has already discussed the issue.

Successful consensus decision making requires the board to discuss an issue thoroughly before voting. This will include conflict, but it's okay for board members to disagree on an issue. Often disagreement serves to rescue the board from making a bad decision. Far too often the pastor or a board patriarch pushes for a decision that's wrong. Poor boardsmanship means going along with a bad or wrong decision for the sake of unity or because the pastor or leader encourages it. Good boardsmanship means challenging such decisions.

The problem is the fear of conflict. Few want to debate with another board member or the pastor. However, a culture where there is freedom to challenge a decision is the kind of culture that breeds good board leadership. I suspect that this is also a trust issue. We risk conflict with others to the degree that we trust them. This is a vulnerability-based trust. We're more willing to differ with and debate those whom we trust than those whom we don't trust. It may appear that boards that experience little disagreement and debate are good boards, that they are unified. However, these boards may simply not trust one another and not be willing to risk healthy debate and disagreement.

For consensus decisions, the board members agree to support the final decision of the team even if they disagree with it. They agree to disagree. At the end, all should be able to say that they either agree with the decision or at least had their day in court. In the final analysis, all agree to support the outcome as if there were no disagreement. The idea is to pursue unity but not unanimity (see Eph. 4:1–13). Should those who oppose a decision feel that the stakes are too high and there is no way that they can support the majority position, they should consider resigning from the board. However, it's imperative that they not discuss this matter with others, cause a disturbance, attempt to rally support for their position outside the board, or work against the board in any way.

Once the board has established its policies, it will use them, in turn, to guide all further decisions affecting the church.

For further information that will help you with the concept of consensus decision making, see Glenn Parker's *Team Players and Teamwork*, pages 44–45; Carver and Carver's *Reinventing Your Board*, page 168; and Malphurs's *Advanced Strategic Planning*, pages 35–36.[4]

Questions for Reflection and Discussion

1. Are you familiar with the policies approach to leadership developed by John Carver? Is the fact that he writes for and works primarily with groups that aren't necessarily Christian a problem for you? If so, why? (If so, go back and read the early part of the Introduction where I discuss this issue under special and natural revelation.)
2. Does the policies approach to board leadership make good sense to you? Why or why not? What do you like or dislike about it?
3. The author addresses eleven advantages for the policies approach. Which would be advantages for your board situation? Which wouldn't?
4. The author is a strong proponent of consensus decision making. Can you explain it? What is the alternative? Does your board decide issues by consensus or compromise? Why?
5. What is the distinction between ministry ends and means? Which would characterize the ministry of your pastor and any staff? Which characterizes the ministry of your board?

BOARD POLICIES

Areas for Board Leadership

As stated in the last chapter, the board will use consensus to develop its policies in at least four areas: the board's ministry, the senior pastor's ministry, the board–senior pastor relationship, and the church's mission and vision. John Carver would argue that all church policies should fall into one of these four areas.[1] In this chapter I will address these four areas in some depth.

Policies Governing the Board

The board's model of governance is found in the policies it drafts to govern itself. This is the process through which the board fulfills its leadership commitment to the congregation or to itself, depending on the church's polity. These policies provide standards for group and individual performance and serve as a constant guide for new board members as well as for established board members.

As Carver teaches, policy governance places the right to interpret these policies primarily in the hands of the board chairperson and anyone else to whom the board explicitly delegates the responsibility.[2] (This is often true of the policies that govern the board's relationship to the senior pastor.) This would appear to give the chairperson unlimited power, which in the hands of the wrong person could lead to board domination. However, the board chairperson leads and interprets policy under

---

*These policies provide standards for group
and individual performance.*

---

the scrutiny of the other board members. Should there be a problem, the board can make policy to cover the issue and rein in the board chairperson.

If the board doesn't have a chairperson, the leader who functions in that role (senior pastor or other) has the right to interpret the policies. (That's why having the pastor serve as chairperson scares some people. It would mean that a lot of power at the board leadership level would be concentrated in the pastor's hands. However, the board can rein him in as they would any chairperson.)

Drafting Individual Board Policies

You have several options in drafting your board policies. The one you choose will depend much on the creative makeup of your team. One option is to start fresh and create your own policies from scratch. This would take the longest and consume the most time. Another is to start with an existing example that will give you some ideas of how to word your own. I have placed such an example of what a set of board policies might look like in appendix C, and appendices K–N provide additional examples of how some churches both small and large have formulated their policies. Though they are found in the appendix, they provide important information, and you may want to start your drafting process with them by discussing their implications for your board and revising them to suit your situation. Assign some of the board members to read through these samples and bring to the group any insight they gain from them.

Carver advises that you start by writing the most general, most inclusive policy. He calls this level 1.[3] In this policy the board decides and then articulates what its function is. The following is an example of a possible level 1 policy.

Level 1: Board Function Policy. The purpose of the board, on behalf of the congregation (if congregational rule), is to make sure that the church pursues its mission, protects its essential biblical doctrines (faith), and observes biblical standards (practice).

First level policies are purposefully broad and open to a wide range of interpretations. If the board feels that it needs to provide more information to limit or guide the board chairperson when interpreting this policy, it needs to move to the next level (level 2), which builds on level 1. It would seem wise that the board move at least to level 2 to give the chairperson a better idea of its expectations of the board. The following are typical second level board topics:

- Board job description (what the board does—its functions or roles)
- Board members' qualifications—the qualifications for being on and staying on the board. In addition to clear biblical qualifications, the policy should state whether board members can be divorced, drink alcoholic beverages, and so forth.
- Board members' conduct—the moral responsibilities of the individual members
- Operations—how the board carries out its business
- Chairperson's role—the chairperson's responsibilities
- Board committee principles—the functions of and rules for using committees
- Board monitoring and evaluation—how the board will monitor itself
- Board training—how board members will improve as leaders
- Choosing a senior pastor
- Determining the senior pastor's compensation and benefits
- Senior pastor emergency succession

If the board decides that it wants to refine these points even further, it would be moving to level 3 policies, which would build on level 2 (see

---

First level policies are purposefully broad and open to a wide range of interpretations.

---

example in appendix C). The board must determine at what level it is satisfied with letting its chairperson interpret the policy. If the board wants more specificity in the policies, it must write them at a higher level.

The board will need to draft its policies, then discuss and even debate them, changing or adding to them as necessary until it reaches consensus.

Policies Governing the Senior Pastor

The relationship between the board and the senior pastor has proved to be one of the most important relationships in the church. Not only is it important that the board be involved in recruiting and selecting a good senior pastor, it must be able to work well with this person, which should encourage his effective spiritual leadership. A poor relationship with the board means the pastor won't be around very long. As Carver points out, essentially the board has only one employee—in our case, the

> *The relationship between the board and the senior pastor has proved to be one of the most important relationships in the church.*

senior pastor.[4] He's equal to any other board person, and no single board member has authority over him (this defuses the guardian of the gate, the renegade, or the bully board person). Yet the pastor is accountable to the full board for himself, the staff, and all that takes place under his leadership. When something goes wrong, he is the responsible party. The board is responsible for developing policies that govern and direct the senior pastor and through him the staff (means policies). And the senior pastor is responsible for interpreting these policies.

What the Policies Accomplish

The policies governing the senior pastor accomplish two things. First, the policies that address the pastor's role will tell him what the board wants him to accomplish, specifically spelling out what the senior pastor should achieve. John Carver would not agree. He believes that the policies affecting the CEO (senior pastor) should be only limitations policies that spell out what he *can't* do, which ultimately frees him to accomplish much more than normal.[5] However, unlike the corporate and public not-for-profit worlds, there are certain biblical directives that

affect a pastor's ministry, things he must or should do. And these are
spelled out rather clearly in such prescriptive passages as Acts 20:28;
1 Timothy 5:17; 2 Timothy 4:2; and others. Thus I argue that board
policies affecting the senior pastor should not only limit what he can
do but also address what he *must* do according to Scripture. There are
just a few specifics that must be addressed by the board.

Second, some policies will restrict the pastor. They will set certain
boundaries or limits for him and the staff. These are meant to be restric-
tive, though this may seem negative. Just the opposite is true, however;
and therein lies the genius of the policies governance approach as developed by Carver. Telling the pastor what he and the staff can't do (as
well as a few things they must do) frees them up to do more than if
the board attempts to tell him *all* that they can do. In limiting them in
a few areas, the board grants much freedom to make decisions. It's an
extremely empowering approach.

It's imperative that the board understand that whatever doesn't violate
board policies is automatically board authorized. If the board hasn't
said that the pastor can't do something, then he *can* do it. Should this
become problematic in some area, the board will need to draft policy
covering that matter.

Drafting Pastor Policies

To begin drafting a policy for the pastor, state the general, most inclusive policy—level 1. It should be broad enough to cover all possible
actions and considerations of the senior pastor. The following is an
example of a level 1 policy for a senior pastor: *The senior pastor will lead*

---

*A level 1 policy for the pastor should be broad enough to cover
all possible actions and considerations of the senior pastor.*

---

*the congregation by protecting it from false doctrine (Acts 20:28), teaching
it the Scriptures (1 Tim. 5:17), and directing its activities (1 Tim. 5:17),
including the supervision of all staff.*

In drafting this policy statement, the board will have wrestled with
such things as its content, meaning, wording, and length. It will have
discussed and voted to approve it. It is wise not to address how the senior pastor will do his job; he should know that better than the board.
If he doesn't or the board has to tell him how to do his ministry, then

the board has hired the wrong person. Unfortunately, this is often the case with recent seminary graduates who have focused *only* on knowing the Bible, theology, and preaching and teaching the Bible.

Next, the board must consider what level of interpretation by the senior pastor it will accept. Will it accept any reasonable interpretation? If the answer is yes, the board will move on to the next policy. However, most boards conclude that it's wise to include more specifics and write the policy at least at level 2.

Level 2 policies build on level 1 and further define them. If the board moves to level 2 on the policy governing the senior pastor, the following are some topics that it might consider as areas of board concern (you can see these fleshed out in appendix D):

- pastor's job description (the board's expectations of him)
- pastor's board responsibilities (how the pastor serves the board)
- pastor's code of conduct (the pastor's moral responsibilities)
- pastor's financial management (how the pastor handles finances)
- pastor's assets management (how the pastor manages the church's assets)
- pastoral committees (what role and power committees have)
- pastor's retirement (the pastor's relationship to the church and board after retirement)
- pastor's emergency succession (what happens if the pastor leaves)

The board must determine if written policies on all or any of these are needed and if anything is missing. There may be something unique to the nature of your ministry that needs to be included here. If the board decides that it wants to refine these even further, it would develop level 3 policies.

As with the board policies, you have several options in drafting your policies governing the senior pastor. Again, you may prefer to create your own from scratch. However, if you want to work from an existing model, refer to the one in appendix D, which will help you accurately accommodate your unique ministry.

Special note: Before leaving this section, I need to address the typical board's approach to finances. Since most boards believe that they must approve all line items in their budget (most of which they know little about), the following, based on Carver's thinking, should prove helpful.[6]

Rather than approve the actual budget, the board sets policies or guidelines that the pastor and his staff use to construct the budget so that policies drive the budget instead of the budget driving the policies. This gives the senior pastor freedom to use funds wisely. As the fiscal year progresses, he may have to shift some funds. With this approach, he doesn't have to go back to the board for permission each time he does so. The board's concerns aren't about the budget but the actual fiscal state of the ministry. For an example of this, see the statement about the budget in appendix D under Pastor's Financial Management.

Policies Governing the Board–Senior Pastor Relationship

The board uses ministry means policies to describe how it transfers a large portion of its authority to the senior pastor. They don't attempt to tell the senior pastor how to do his job. The policies explain how the board will work with or relate to the senior pastor. They don't describe what the board delegates to the senior pastor (policies governing the

---

The board uses ministry means policies to describe how it transfers a large portion of its authority to the senior pastor.

---

senior pastor) but rather how that delegation occurs. Since these policies address who has power in the church, I suggest that you review appendix J, which explores this concept more in depth.

As with the other policies above, begin at level 1 to draft these policies, stating the general, most inclusive policy first. It should be broad enough to cover all possible actions and considerations. The following is an example of a level 1 policy for the board–senior pastor relationship: *The board corporately entrusts the senior pastor with the authority to be the primary leader of the church and its ministry.*

Most boards would want to expand on this statement and take it to level 2. If the board moves to level 2, the following are some topics that it might consider as areas of board focus (you can see examples in appendix E):

- pastor's authority (the pastor's authority as primary leader of the church)

- pastor's accountability (what the board holds the pastor accountable for)
- pastor's direction (policies that direct what the pastor does and doesn't do)
- pastor's monitoring and evaluation (done by the board)
- pastor's advising (the board's responsibility to the pastor)

At this point, the board must decide if all or any of these are needed and if anything is missing. Perhaps there is something unique to the nature of your ministry that needs to be included. If the board decides that it wants to refine these even further, it should next move to level 3. Most boards go at least to level 3.

I want to encourage you to be creative in developing the policies that cover the relationship between your board and senior pastor. The sample in appendix E may help you develop your own. In addition, you may want to refer to the policy statements of a small church and several larger churches in appendices K–N as further examples of what some churches have done to develop their policies.

Policies Governing the Church's Mission

The board's primary responsibility is to monitor and hold the church to its mission—that is the Great Commission (Matt. 28:19–20). If the church doesn't have a mission, it must develop one. Otherwise it has no direction. Should the church already have a mission, it should regularly review it.

This will be at the very heart of the board's work, because it is the ministry ends or mission that justifies having a church in the first place.

The board's primary responsibility is to monitor and hold the church to its mission—that is the Great Commission (Matt. 28:19–20). This will be at the very heart of the board's work.

It's the board's never-ending task to determine what the church is supposed to be doing—its mission—and seeing that it does it (monitoring). This is what some mean when they talk about ends policies. The mission is the mega end result for the organization's existence. It is what directs the senior pastor and the board to know where it wants the church to go—its ministry mission. It's the purpose for the church.

The mission is both outward focused (evangelism) and inward focused (edification), according to Matthew 28:19–20 and other Great Commission passages. The board should work to see that the two are balanced, which probably means emphasizing evangelism over edification. It's far more difficult to reach out than it is to reach in. If the church emphasizes edification instead of or over evangelism, it will begin to die.

The mission also states who will benefit from the church and in what way. For example, who is the church's target group? Where are they located? Choosing a target group may prove to be difficult, maybe even painful, because by determining whom you will reach, you also determine whom you are likely not to reach. The truth is, however, that you can't reach everybody.

Establishing Mission Policies

Should the church establish mission policies? This might seem like a strange question at this point in the policies developing process. However, the answer to this question depends on whether the board has addressed this issue in another context. For example, in my book *Advanced Strategic Planning*, I insist that churches that are going through the strategic planning process develop a mission statement that determines where they are going in ministry (the directional component) and what they are supposed to be doing (the functional component). Consequently, churches that have taken time to develop a clear, compelling mission statement as a part of their strategic thinking may not need, at this point, to establish mission policies. If the church doesn't have a mission statement, however, it's imperative that it develop one. It may do so at this point as it develops its governance policies, or it would be wise to enlist a competent consultant and work its way through a good strategic planning process that helps it discover its core values and develop a mission and vision as well as a disciple-making strategy.[7]

Drafting Your Mission Policies

To draft your mission policies, first, state the mission. The following is one of many possible mission statements that I'll use to illustrate the process: *Our mission is to make and mature believers at home and abroad.*

Next, decide if there are any aspects of the mission that the board wants to define more narrowly, thus limiting the senior pastor's latitude for interpreting and implementing the mission. The following illustrates ways to further develop the mission:

> *Making believers:* This involves winning lost people to faith in Christ. Who are these lost people? Who are you most likely to reach in your community?
>
> *Maturing believers:* These are saved people. Who are these people? Are they the current congregation? Anyone else?
>
> *At home:* Is this a reference to your ministry community? Where is that community? What are its boundaries?
>
> *Abroad:* Where does *abroad* mean? Is this your international outreach? Where will you go internationally? Where will you not go?

You will need to subject these items to analysis or debate within the board. The board members may need time to think about them, due to the importance of the mission statement to the church's ministry. Once all this has taken place, vote on them and begin to implement them.

There is a sample of a mission policy in appendix F. Please scan it and use it if you think it might be helpful in developing your own.

Using the Policies

Once your board has drafted its policies, it needs to preserve and make them available to the board members, because much of what the board does when it meets is based on these policies. In particular, the board will be making lots of decisions—one of its functions. Hardly a board meeting takes place that it doesn't have to make decisions. A primary purpose

---

Much of what the board does when it meets is based on these policies.

---

of these policies is to guide them in their decision making. In a policies approach, they will be either applying or revising existing policies or establishing new ones in practically every meeting. To accomplish this, the board must have access to the policies already written.

I suggest that the policies be placed in some kind of notebook. The board chairperson, the pastor, or an administrative assistant should be sure that each board person has one. Depending on the business to be conducted, board persons should bring their notebooks to the board meetings. It's a good idea to have extra copies available at the meeting site for those who forget to bring them. Another option would be to put all the policies on the computer and devise a system similar to Google whereby the board could enter a word or two and access the appropriate policy or perhaps discover that a policy has not been written in a particular area.

Questions for Reflection and Discussion

1. Do you agree that most governance policies should fall within one of the four covered in this chapter? If not, what would be an exception?
2. In designing the policies for your board, pastor, board–senior pastor relationship, and mission, will you use the sample policies located in appendices C–F as a guide? Why or why not?
3. What additional topics would you include in your four policies that aren't covered in the samples in appendices C–F?
4. Will you include mission policies in your policies development? Why or why not?
5. When will you begin as a board to develop your governance policies?

10

BOARD MEETINGS

One of the requirements for any board is that board members attend its meetings if anything of consequence is to happen. The problem is that the meetings take time, and most of us have little time. Nonetheless, boards have to meet to serve their ministry.

This chapter addresses the question, How will the board meet? It focuses on three particular issues that involve using a policies approach. These issues are preparing for board meetings, determining the content of those meetings, and conducting a typical board meeting.

Preparing for Board Meetings

In preparing for board meetings there are several concerns: the frequency of meetings, their length, the meeting agenda, and meeting minutia.

Frequency of Meetings

The first order of business is to determine the frequency of board meetings. For most churches, the frequency of meetings depends on tradition rather than careful planning. Ask why a board meets when it does, and you'll be greeted with blank stares or the statement: "We've always done it that way." Tradition will vary from church to church. I suspect, however, that the majority of boards meet once or twice a month with some time off in the summer.

The frequency with which leaders meet should depend on a number of issues. One is how involved the board wants to be in leading the leaders. Less involvement requires less time in meetings. A second issue that ties closely to the first is the board's function or role, such as praying, deciding, monitoring, and other roles. A third issue is the church's circumstances. The board might meet more often if the senior pastor is new to the church or the church is going through a difficult time. A fourth issue is the relationship of frequency to the length of meetings. The group may prefer to meet more frequently for shorter periods of time, such as twice a month for two to three hours, or it may want to meet less often for longer periods of time, such as once a month for four to six hours. It should be remembered that if a board meets too frequently, it tends to slip into a monotonous routine that is rarely meaningful. But if it doesn't meet often enough, time is required at each meeting to remind members of what they've done, what needs to be done, and where they're going. So if your leaders are experiencing either extreme, you know that the board has a frequency problem and must make some vital, midcourse corrections.

The answer to the question of frequency is that each board must decide based on its own circumstances and people. The key issue that I want to stress is that the board must discuss and decide this issue at least annually (it could change from year to year) as opposed to ignoring the issue entirely and falling back on tradition.

Length of Meetings

The amount of time that boards take for their meetings varies considerably. The particular circumstances of the church should dictate this matter, as discussed above. However, the average lay church-governing board devotes no more than four to six hours a month to board meetings. Regardless of the church's size or the board members' demographics, most board members have busy schedules. Therefore, it is wiser to extend board meetings by several hours to get the work accomplished than to schedule extra meetings.

With a policies approach to board ministry, most leaders find that they don't have to deal with minutiae, so meeting time can be spent on important issues, which ultimately saves time and makes the meetings more worthwhile.

Meeting Agenda

With limited time and expertise, what should be on the agenda when the board meets? The obvious answer is business that is important to the church, often relating to the church's mission or ministry ends. In other words the "bet the company" issues, those that, if not properly addressed, could cause the ministry to fail.

The reality is that well-meaning boards deal with everything and anything that is brought to their attention or that a board member wishes to discuss, whether or not it's important to the church as a whole. This is especially true of that which is deemed urgent. One way to care for this is to reserve at least half or more of every board meeting to focus on the most important matters, which means setting aside enough time for thorough exploration of them, fully discussing and interacting with them. Less important issues can be discussed in the time remaining.

Meeting Minutiae

Boards that attempt to address anything and everything become immersed in minutiae (dabbling in the details). To make matters worse, the board may spend considerable time discussing one or two trivial items and get even further behind. The result is longer-than-necessary meetings that deal largely with matters that won't make much of a difference in the life of the church. In addition, board members may leave meetings frustrated with how little they have accomplished, which will mean an even longer meeting next time. Good leaders, the kind that you want on a board, will not last long in this kind of culture. They'll sense that they're not making much of a difference and look for more productive ministry opportunities.

Meetings that focus on minutiae usually aren't the fault of any one person, such as the pastor or chairperson of the board. Most likely it's

> *Boards that attempt to address anything and everything become immersed in minutiae.*

church tradition: "Since we've always addressed minutiae, I guess that's what we're supposed to do." If this is the case, it's time for wise leaders to get rid of this kind of thinking about the board's leadership.

The solution to the problem of drowning in minutiae is to address it as a problem. It's possible that somewhere there's a board, comfortable with the status quo, that prefers to do it this way. Before change can take place, the board must acknowledge that this is a serious problem that limits what they can accomplish for the church as leaders. For those that feel this way, the next step is screening the board agenda before the meeting so that only what's board relevant makes the agenda of that meeting. The following three screening questions will help the board chairman and the board to accomplish this.

WHOSE ISSUE IS IT?

The first question is, Whose issue is it? Is this a matter that should come to the board in the first place? Is it a matter for the board or senior pastor or some other staff or layperson? If the answer is that the matter belongs to the staff or the pastor, then it isn't a board agenda item. If no one is sure, then the issue needs further exploration.

Following are several ways to determine who owns the issue.

1. Ask, Does the potential agenda item clearly fall under any of the stated purposes for or functions of the board?
2. Ask, Does it fall under a program, activity, ministry, service, strategy, facilities, or some other ministry means issue? If so, it's a pastor/staff issue.
3. To further clarify the above, ask one or both of the following questions: Is this potential board item a ministry ends or ministry means issue? That is, Does this matter involve an end or a means to an end? If you're not sure, then ask, Is this issue timeless or timely? Timeless issues (such as evangelizing the community) are related to ends and belong to the board, while timely issues (such as the time and place for an evangelistic meeting) are means issues and likely belong to the staff.

Be careful if the senior pastor or any staff are responsible for creating board agendas. Their temptation will be to put staff means issues (staff business) on the board's agenda (board's business).

WHICH POLICY AREA DOES IT FALL UNDER?

Assuming that it's a board issue, the next question is, To which policies category does the issue belong: board, senior pastor, board–senior pastor relationship, or ministry mission?

IS THERE AN EXISTING POLICY?

The final question is, Is there an existing policy that already clarifies or makes the board's decision? If not, the board needs to make policy or revisit a similar policy and further clarify it to deal with the matter at hand.

Content of Board Meetings

When the questions concerning agenda items are answered and only those issues that fall under the board's purview are included on an agenda, much meeting time will be saved. As a result, the board may need to meet only once a month. When it meets, it will be led by a board chairperson or senior pastor who is responsible to see that it accomplishes its ministry. During the meeting, the board will deal with ministry matters that come under its job description. Following are some potential agenda items. Some are primary issues and others will be addressed only on occasion.

1. The board will spend some time in spiritual nurture and prayer for itself, the staff, and the congregation. It may at times pray with these individuals, such as a congregant who requests individual, personal prayer.
2. The board will decide or make policy decisions on matters that fall under the board's functions, the senior pastor's functions, the board–pastor relationship, and the church's mission. This may involve making new policy when necessary or dealing with issues based on existing policies.
3. The board will monitor the church's values, mission, and vision (ministry ends or church DNA). It will determine what these are and hold the church to them. This will involve regularly monitoring these areas.
4. The board will monitor (track and evaluate) the performance of the senior pastor in accomplishing the ministry ends.
5. The board will monitor and evaluate individual board members and the board as a whole.
6. The board will monitor its own ministry and leadership development. It will seek various ways to improve and become a better board.
7. The board will see that new board leaders are oriented to and trained for the board's ministry.
8. The board will decide any issues relating to the constitution and bylaws.
9. The board will arbitrate any disputes with the senior pastor.
10. The board may interview potential future board members.

11. The board will monitor the church's doctrine by interviewing those who will be in teaching positions in the church. This is to make sure that they agree with its faith and practice.
12. The board may license or ordain those that it feels are qualified.
13. The board will monitor and discuss the spiritual condition of the church.
14. The board should deal with any who seek to undermine the ministry of the church or its senior pastor.
15. The board may monitor staff and congregational morale and retention.
16. The board may monitor board and leadership development.
17. The board may assess and monitor the church's image in the community.
18. The board may measure the church's vulnerability to risk.

A Typical Board Agenda

Prayer and spiritual nurture
Make policies
Address the church's DNA
Pastor evaluation
Self-evaluation
Board development
New board member training
Constitution and bylaws issues
Arbitrate disputes with pastor
Potential board member interviews
Church teacher interviews
Licensure and ordination
Monitor the church's spiritual condition
Church discipline
Monitor staff and congregational morale and retention
Monitor board and leadership development
Assess and monitor the church's image in the community
Measure the church's vulnerability to risk

Conducting a Board Meeting

Robust Dialogue

How will you handle or discuss what's on the board's agenda? Probably much of what a board does is to discuss matters and make decisions based on its policies. The key to doing this well is robust dialogue. In *Execution: The Discipline of Getting Things Done*, Larry Bossidy says, "You cannot have an execution culture without robust dialogue—one that brings reality to the surface through openness, candor, and informality."[1]

The goal of robust dialogue is to discuss the issues with open minds, bringing in any new information, listening to all sides, and choosing the best alternatives for the church that will honor the Savior. There must be no hidden agendas. If discussions are well led, they should regularly involve the board in some debate and differences of opinion. This is necessary to get all the best information in front of the board before it makes a decision or crafts a policy. It's not possible for one person to have all the best ideas or right answers to board issues. It takes a team to probe truth and come to the best decisions. This, however, is more easily described and talked about than accomplished. The problem is that most of us avoid this kind of dialogue because we worry too much about offending someone, having differences of opinion, disrupting board harmony, or experiencing confrontation. After all, Christians don't do these kinds of things, do they?

The truth of the matter is that this says more about our board cultures than we realize. A culture where everyone walks and talks in lockstep with the pastor, chairperson, or benevolent patriarch is spiritually unhealthy. A culture where there's no debate or difference of opinion is spiritually and creatively sterile. Most important, people on these boards don't trust one another (see chapter 6). Have I just described your board culture? Recheck your answer to item 10 on the Governing Board Audit in appendix A. Most believe that the best answer is number 4. Actually, the best answer is number 1.

If you have a problem here (and most do), what can you do to change your board culture? I encourage you to discuss this among the board members. Decide if you really want robust dialogue and debate, because it will make you uncomfortable. Are you ready for this? If not, why not? What does your answer say about your board's health?

A willingness to change to robust dialogue must start at the top, whether this is the pastor, board chairperson, patriarch, matriarch, or some other key leader. This sets the stage for future meetings, determining whether your dialogue will be truly robust. One thing for sure—no one will fall asleep in your meetings or complain that they're boring.

Vulnerability-Based Trust

Leaders of leaders who pursue robust dialogue well trust one another well. But this isn't just any kind of trust—it's a vulnerability-based trust, which means you trust others to the extent that you risk vulnerability with them. Those who are vulnerable are willing to acknowledge their personal mistakes, weaknesses, failures, needs, deficiencies, and so forth. An example is the apostle Paul in Romans 7:14 or 1 Timothy 1:15. The problem is that few of us are willing to do this, because we tend to struggle with competition, self-protection, image, ego, and other similar issues.

To solve this problem, I suggest the following group exercises:

1. Have each board person share with the team his or her personal history and/or testimony (see Paul's in Acts 9; 22; 26). Often vulnerability issues will surface.
2. Have each board member take a church-developed strengths-weaknesses audit (a list of what you believe you're strong and weak at) and share this with the entire team.
3. Identify and discuss your temperament, using the Personal Profile (DiSC) or Myers-Briggs Temperament Indicator (MBTI). This discussion should include typical temperament weaknesses and strengths that are true of most leaders. You can probably obtain these tools from a counseling organization in your community.

In these exercises, it's important to the team that the leader, such as the pastor, lead the way and set the example, which may simply mean going first. I'm convinced that vulnerability-based trust is foundational to robust dialogue and will not happen without it. For further reading, see Patrick Lencioni's excellent presentation on this concept in *The Five Dysfunctions of a Team*.[2]

Questions for Reflection and Discussion

1. How often does your board meet? How often should it meet? What's reasonable for you? On average how much time per month or quarter does your board spend in meetings? Is it more than four to six hours? Would using the policies approach shorten this time? Why or why not?
2. What would be a typical agenda for your board meetings? According to the author, what should not be on the agenda? What should be on it? Would cleaning up the agenda shorten the time the board meets? Why or why not?
3. Does your board often become immersed in ministry minutiae? Why? Did you find the suggestions for avoiding ministry minutiae helpful? Why or why not? How might you implement them?
4. Does your board shy away from any debate or difference of opinion? If so, why? How willing are you to change this and initiate potentially stressful discussions? How willing are you to pursue robust dialogue?
5. Are you as a team person or a board open to pursuing vulnerability-based trust? If so, who will go first?

11

IMPLEMENTING A POLICIES APPROACH

Most leadership boards follow a traditional approach and are unsure how to transition to a policies approach. Some churches that are very small or without a pastor may wonder if the policies approach would work in their situation. This chapter will address these two concerns.

Making the Transition

Following are five steps that will help any board move from a more traditional approach to a policies approach in board governance. I suggest that you take all five steps.

Step 1: Pray for the Board

There's no question that prayer is the most important of the five steps. Anyone who is committed to moving in the direction of a policies approach to leadership must pray for the rest of the board and their responses. We must never underestimate the power of prayer, especially in matters as important as board governance.

In James 5:16 the writer says, "The prayer of a righteous man is powerful and effective." Board leaders must be righteous men who pray. Then in verse 17 James uses Elijah as an example. Elijah prayed that

---

We must never underestimate the power of prayer, especially in matters as important as board governance.

---

it would stop raining, and the rain ceased for three and one-half years. Then he prayed again, and the rain returned. The point is that we, like Elijah, can pray powerful prayers and experience powerful responses, including boards that desire to function more effectively on behalf of the Savior.

Step 2: Take the Board Audit

The Governing Board Audit in appendix A will bring to the surface the problems that the traditional approach poses in leading and operating boards. When I work with churches in such areas as leadership development or strategic planning, I invite those who are on the board to take the audit. For this exercise to be worthwhile, board members

---

Be willing to challenge the traditional ways in which the board has functioned.

---

must express what they really think and not attempt to be protective of the feelings of anyone, such as those who lead the board process.

Because this step is important, you should encourage or even require, if possible, all the board members to take the audit at a regularly scheduled board meeting and then ask them to compare their responses. Be willing to challenge the traditional ways in which the board has functioned.

Step 3: Understand the Policies Governance Approach

Ask the board to read this book or one of John Carver's books on policy governance. If the board sets aside time to work on its development as leaders and board members, this could be one of its assignments.

A further suggestion is that you hire a consultant who knows the policies leadership approach and who will help the board understand it, answer their questions, and even help them through the process of adopting the approach.[1] Initially this might seem like a needless expense. You'll have to determine how important good board governance is to the church and its ministry. You'll only have one shot at this. If it doesn't go well or go at all, there will not be another opportunity. There will always be people around to remind the leaders that they tried that once before, and it didn't work.

Step 4: Make a Commitment to the Approach

If the board sees the wisdom and value of pursuing a policies approach to its governance, it must make a long-term commitment to this approach. It's not a quick fix that can be accomplished overnight or in one brief meeting and will involve some hard work and thinking.

It's not a quick fix that can be accomplished overnight or in one brief meeting.

This can't be a halfhearted response but a total commitment so that the board doesn't go halfway or merely dabble with the policies approach. It's all or nothing.

One idea for helping the board commit to this approach is for the board to assign one of its people—most likely the chairperson or pastor—to be the team accountability person. This individual will take the responsibility to see that the board follows through on its commitment to the approach. He or she will be an accountability gadfly. Like John the Baptist, this person will call the board to repentance should it shirk in any way its commitment to implement the process.

Step 5: Begin the Policies Process

Sometimes a board will agree to pursue the process of developing the policies approach, but the actual pursuit gets lost somewhere along the way. I promise you that there will be all kinds of interruptions to distract you from getting down to God's business. I would like to blame this on Satan, but much of the blame falls at our feet.

Following are several possible tactics you may want to use separately or in combination.

1. Initially you could set aside an hour or more at each board meeting to develop the policies until you have a basic working set in each of the four policy areas for making decisions.
2. Set aside a block of time, such as a Saturday morning or two Saturday mornings, to design the policies.
3. Get away on a weekend board retreat to establish the initial working policies.

Steps for Making the Transition to a Policies Approach

Step 1: Pray for the board.
Step 2: Take the board audit and discuss the results.
Step 3: Understand the policies governance approach.
Step 4: Ask the board to make a commitment to the approach.
Step 5: Begin the policies approach.

Special Circumstances

The Policies Approach and Small Churches

According to *Faith Communities in the United States Today*, one-half of congregations have fewer than one hundred regularly attending adults, and a full quarter of congregations have fewer than fifty regularly participating adults. Consequently, a significant number of churches are small churches. The question is, how does the policies approach work with these small churches that have few if any staff?

When the pastor of a small church—often the sole staff person—is bivocational or has not attended seminary, the board may believe, even assume, that he doesn't have the necessary resources to lead the church well. Even if this is the case, the board that is following the policies ap-

---

Lay governing boards must resist the temptation to push themselves and their opinions on the pastor. This is strictly out of bounds for the governing board.

---

proach should not involve themselves in the pastor's area of ministry (ministry means). The pastor and any staff that pursue the church's mission (ends policies) within the policies governing the pastor will determine what help he or they may need. The board should not decide this. (If the pastor can't figure this out, perhaps he shouldn't be the pastor.)

The pastor is free to ask individual board members to assist or offer advice. If this happens, these board members are acting strictly as individuals and volunteers under the authority of the pastor not as board members representing the board or holding board power. However, the governing board is not free to help or advise the pastor and staff unless they request it. These lay governing boards must resist the temptation to push themselves and their opinions on the pastor. This is strictly out of bounds for the governing board.

The Policies Approach and Churches without a Pastor

How does the policies approach work in the church that is without a senior pastor? As I have said, most churches will have a new pastor every three to four years. This results in periods of time when the church is either without a pastor or ministers with an interim pastor. Some churches are so small that they can't afford a pastor. Does the policies approach work for them?

WEARING TWO HATS

The policies approach will work in these situations. However, the board must temporarily pursue the separate roles of board and of staff, wearing two hats in the church. While wearing the board hat, the board continues to function as the board—praying, monitoring, deciding, and advising.

While wearing the staff hat, the board and others may function as staff, doing much or all of the staff's work, such as making decisions about and carrying out the daily operations of the church. The problem is that the board while acting in place of staff will allow the urgency of operating the church (the staff role) to distract it from focusing on the mission or ministry ends (the board's role). It must clearly discern between the two hats—the hat of governance and the hat of pastor and staff—and place priority on the former since that is its chief responsibility.

AN IDEAL TIME

Actually, an ideal time to implement a policies approach to board leadership is when a church is in a pastoral search mode. Thus, when it locates a viable candidate, the board can clearly articulate its expectations of the pastor (Policies Governing the Pastor) as well as itself (Policies

---

An ideal time to implement a policies approach to board leadership is when a church is in a pastoral search mode.

Governing the Board) and the lines of authority between itself and the pastor (Policies Governing the Board–Senior Pastor Relationship) in the exercise of power.

A WARNING

Once the church has a pastor, the board must resist the temptation to continue to operate as staff and call the shots. It must be the board and let the new pastor be the pastor. This doesn't mean that individual board members can't help the pastor, but this must occur only at his bidding. It does mean that the board trades in its staff hat and goes back to wearing only its board hat.

Questions for Reflection and Discussion

1. Would all five steps for implementing a policies approach work for your board? Why or why not? Can you think of some additional steps that the author doesn't mention?
2. Which of the three tactics suggested would help your board begin to implement a policies approach? Why? Can you think of some other tactics that the author doesn't mention that would be helpful to you?
3. Is your church a small church (under one hundred)? If so, is there any reason why the board couldn't implement such an approach?
4. Why does the author feel that, when a church is without a pastor, it is a good time for a church to implement a policies governance approach? Do you agree? If so, can you think of any other good reasons why this is a good time for implementing the approach? If you disagree, what might be the dangers?

12

IMPROVING BOARD EFFECTIVENESS
Training Board Leadership

I n this final chapter, I'll spend less time on the policies concept and turn our attention to board development. Because leaders are learners, the board must invest in and participate in its training on an ongoing basis. The purpose is to assist the board in becoming more effective as leaders.

A major reason so many boards are struggling in their leadership is that neither established board members nor new board members have

---

Because leaders are learners, the board must invest in and participate in its training on an ongoing basis.

---

been trained. While this entire book is training material, the following will focus attention on four critical core developmental competencies—character, knowledge, skills, and emotions.

The Leader's Character (Soul Work)

Is Character Important?

The first core competency is character. It affects the very heart and soul of the leader and is foundational to the other core competencies. It is soul work that develops the leader's Christlikeness. Psalm 78:72

Any church's governance board should seek to be people with integrity of heart.

---

says that David shepherded (led) his people with "integrity of heart." Any church's governance board should seek to be people with integrity of heart. However, like so many other important things in life, leaders must work at their character—it won't develop overnight.

Development Area 1

Character (being)	Soul Work

Character Qualities

The importance of character (being) raises the key question of who leaders must be to lead effectively at the board level. What are the character requirements for board people? Scripture provides us with some general character qualities in 1 Timothy 3:1–7; Titus 1:6–9; and 1 Peter 5:2. I have developed a character audit using the first two references, which I'll say more about below. Acts 6:3–5 provides some qualities for early church leaders, and Galatians 5:22–23 identifies the fruit of the Spirit.

Some other necessary character qualities are referred to in 2 Timothy 2:2. These include competence, trustworthiness, and teachability. I consider teachability vital. A lack of teachability is the potential leader's disqualification, because leaders must always be learners. Should they stop learning, they stop leading. If one is unteachable at the beginning, he or she isn't leadership material, because at the heart of those who aren't teachable is personal pride immersed in arrogance (see Prov. 8:13; 16:18; 1 Tim. 3:6).

Assessing Character Qualities

I have developed two character audits that I use in training leaders at the seminary and church levels. Both are in the appendices. One is

for male leadership (appendix G) and is based on the character qualities in 1 Timothy 3:1–7 and Titus 1:6–9. The other is for women leaders
(appendix H) and is based on 1 Timothy 2:9–10; 3:11; Titus 2:3–5; and
1 Peter 3:1–4. Board leaders should find these audits helpful in assess-
ing the character of leaders.

The Leader's Knowledge (Headwork)

Is Knowledge Important?

The second core competency involves the leader's intellect or knowledge. Whereas the leader's character is soul work that addresses his very
being, knowledge involves headwork, addressing his intellect. It's the
cognitive aspect of learning and emphasizes the ability to acquire and

---

Leaders must have knowledge of their ministry areas.

---

process content or information that influences the leader's life and that
of his followers. This information may be old or new. Regardless, leaders
must have knowledge of their ministry areas. In God's preparation of
Moses for leadership, he specifically taught him what to do. In Exodus
4:15 God says of Aaron and Moses, "I will help both of you speak and
will teach you what to do."

Development Area 2

Knowledge (knowing)	Headwork

Necessary Knowledge Components

What must one know to lead at the board level? What are the basic
knowledge requirements at each leadership level? There is certain information that leaders must know and other information that it would be
helpful to know. To identify all the knowledge components for leaders
at the board level is beyond the scope of this book, but here are some
general guidelines:

1. They must know God and how to walk in the Spirit to lead at the
   board level.
2. They must know how to study the Bible and have a general knowledge of the Bible and theology to recognize and challenge false
   teaching.

3. They must know how to pray as they must pray for themselves, the congregation, the pastor, and staff.
4. They must know and agree with the organization's statements (core values, mission, vision, strategy, and beliefs or doctrine).
5. They need to know themselves and people (the divine design concept).
6. They need to know how to think and act strategically.
7. They need to know and understand the contents of this book in general and board policies in particular.

Acquiring Knowledge

There are numerous ways that the board might approach the knowledge component. They could read and discuss various books that supply needed leadership information. For example, the elder board that I serve with at my church read through John Carver's book *Boards That Make a Difference* to help us better function as a board. We also read Charles Ryrie's *A Survey of Bible Doctrine* to firm up our knowledge of theology and the Bible. In addition, we attended a Willow Creek leadership conference.

The Leader's Skills (Handwork)

Are Leadership Skills Important?

The third core competency is the leader's skills. They affect the leader's actions or behavior. Character concerns his soul work, and knowledge addresses headwork. Skills involve his handwork, which enables doing.

Psalm 78:72 says that David led his people not only with "integrity of heart" but with "skillful hands." Leaders must be able to put into practice

---

Leaders must be able to put into practice what they learn.

---

what they learn. Having a knowledge of leadership is not enough. They must be able to lead, turning theory into practice.

Development Area 2

Skills (doing)	Handwork

Necessary Leadership Skills

There are certain key skills that enable a person to function well as a governing board leader. Following are some general skills.

Hard Skills

Hard or task skills include knowing how to cast vision, pray, discover and develop core ministry values, develop a ministry mission statement and strategy, teach and preach the Bible or a Sunday school lesson. Especially for the board member, they include the skill of policy development and policy implementation.

Soft Skills

The soft or relational skills include knowing how to listen, encourage, mentor or coach, resolve conflicts, network, counsel, motivate, take risks, solve problems, build trust, make good decisions, build effective teams, recruit, tell stories, confront, be creative, think strategically, and do other vital ministry tasks.

The Leader's Emotions (Heart Work)

Are the Leader's Emotions Important?

Simply stated, emotions are one's feelings. The leader's emotions are the leader's heart work, reflecting what he or she feels. Scripture has much to say about emotions. For example, Adam and Eve experienced shame when they sinned (Gen. 3:9–11 compared to 2:22). Cain struggled with anger (4:1–8), and Moses "lost it" while leading the Israelites (Exod. 32:19). Jesus openly expressed sadness at the death of Lazarus (John 11:33–35, 38).

The leader's emotions are critical for his or her own spiritual well-being and that of others. This is why I haven't included them under

---

The leader's emotions are critical for his or her own spiritual well-being and that of others.

---

character or skills where they might also fit. A board person's emotions affect his or her mood. Research indicates that the leader's mood is contagious, spreading quickly throughout the organization. A good mood (one characterized by optimism, authenticity, energy, and inspiration) affects the board and ministry most positively. However, a bad mood (one characterized by negativity, pessimism, fear, anxiety, humiliation, harshness, and grouchiness) will cripple ministry and damage people.

Development Area 4

Emotions (feeling)   Heart work

Cultivating Emotional Well-Being

To develop emotional well-being and establish a healthy mood for their ministry, board leaders would be wise to cultivate two primary areas—understanding and managing their own emotions and recognizing and managing the emotions of others.

The following steps will help leaders understand their emotions:

1. They should try to recognize their emotions when they experience them.
2. Once leaders learn to recognize their emotions, they should identify them by asking, What emotion am I experiencing? Some of the primary negative core emotions to look for are anger, anxiety, sadness, fear, shame, discouragement, guilt, greed, despair, envy, hate, pride, grief, and loneliness.
3. When leaders recognize their emotions, they can begin to deal with them. While it isn't wrong to experience an emotion, some emotions, such as anger, must be dealt with quickly, or they may become problematic (Eph. 4:26–27). Other potentially problematic emotions are discouragement, sadness, fear, shame, and pessimism.

Not only should leaders be aware of their emotions and the moods they set for the ministry, they also need to recognize others' emotions and ensuing moods. This is commonly referred to as empathy. Most of

> *Not only should leaders be aware of their emotions and the moods they set for the ministry; they also need to recognize others' emotions and ensuing moods.*

us have been in situations where an emotionally unhealthy person negatively affects a ministry, even though he or she is not a leader. This is often true in board contexts. It's imperative that leaders deal with such a person for the sake of the ministry as well as the individual. Leaders can accomplish this in much the same way they work with their own emotions, applying the three steps above to others.

Leadership Development Areas

Character (being)	Soul Work
Knowledge (knowing)	Headwork
Skills (doing)	Handwork
Emotions (feeling)	Heart Work

I have written two other books on leadership—the first two parts of a trilogy that includes this work. These should prove most beneficial to developing board leaders. *Being Leaders* helps leaders think through what leadership is. It seeks to define and get at the very nature of leadership. When we talk about leaders and leadership, who and what are we talking about? Are we even on the same page? *Building Leaders* addresses at a greater depth the issues covered in this chapter. Will Mancini and I designed this work to equip you with a process to develop leaders, not only at the upper levels of your church but at every ministry level of your church.

Questions for Reflection and Discussion

1. The author suggests that board leaders develop in at least four areas (character, knowledge, skills, and emotions). Do you agree? If not, why not? Are there some other areas that you would suggest for the development of your board?
2. Of the four areas, is one more important to your board than the others? If so, which one? Why?
3. What are the character qualifications if any for your board? Are they based on Scripture? If not, why not? If so, which passages?
4. Does the board meet these character qualifications? How would you know? Did they take the character audit in the appendices? If not, why not?
5. What specifically does a board member need to know to function effectively on your board?
6. What specifically does a board member need to be able to do to function effectively on your board?
7. How would you describe the emotional climate in which the board works? Does it need to be changed? If so, what would you recommend?

GOVERNING BOARD AUDIT

One of the most influential leadership groups in your church is the governing board. How is your board doing? Circle the answer that best describes your board situation.

	True	More true than false	More false than true	False
1. I feel that my work on the board is a most valuable use of my time.	1	2	3	4
2. The board addresses the most important issues that affect our church.	1	2	3	4
3. The board doesn't micromanage the church and its ministry.	1	2	3	4
4. The board has a clear, compelling direction.	1	2	3	4
5. I feel that my work on the board is a good use of my gifts and abilities.	1	2	3	4
6. The board doesn't spend time on trivial matters.	1	2	3	4
7. No one person dominates or tries to control the board.	1	2	3	4
8. The board is performing at a high percentage of its leadership potential.	1	2	3	4

9. The board is proactive not reactive in its work.	1	2	3	4
10. The board members often disagree and debate with one another.	1	2	3	4
11. New board members receive an orientation and training for their position.	1	2	3	4
12. The board members trust and show respect for one another.	1	2	3	4
13. The board members are well qualified spiritually for the board's work.	1	2	3	4
14. The board has set clear lines of authority between itself and the pastor.	1	2	3	4
15. By being on the board, I am making a significant difference for Christ.	1	2	3	4
16. I am disappointed when board meetings are canceled.	1	2	3	4
17. The board has established a clear set of policies that guide its decisions.	1	2	3	4
18. It is rare that board meetings last for more than two hours.	1	2	3	4
19. All items that appear on the board's agenda have been carefully screened by the board chairperson.	1	2	3	4
20. Rarely do board members interfere with the staff's work.	1	2	3	4

Directions for scoring: Add up all the numbers that you circled.

Total score: _____

If your score is

> 20–34: You have an excellent board.
> 35–49: You have an above average board the closer your score is to 35.
> 50–65: You have a below average board, especially the closer your score is to 65.
> 66–80: You have a dysfunctional board.

If your board didn't score well, we can help. Contact The Malphurs Group (amalphurs@dts.edu).

THE ROLE OF A BOARD MEMBER'S SPOUSE

The spouse of a church board member plays an important part in the board member's ministry, often determining its effectiveness. The spouse should be aware of the following ways in which he or she is able to minister to the board member.

- Your spouse must have your full support. He or she has been chosen to serve in this role and you must faithfully stand with him or her.
- You have a spiritual responsibility to pray for your spouse. Your spiritual support is essential to his or her successful leadership in the body of Christ.
- Disunity in the home means a weak spiritual life, which, in turn, means a weak link in the leadership of the church.
- You and your family are examples, and you now have certain expectations that you may not have considered before. Remember that your attitude speaks louder than your words.
- There may be times when your spouse is aware of things that he or she is not at liberty to share with you at the moment. You must

pray with him or her without knowing all the facts. There will be times when you are aware of things that the congregation is not. You are expected to remain free from gossip and in an attitude of prayer.

- Sometimes others may approach you to tell you things to pass on to your spouse so that he or she will tell the pastor. You are not the listening post for your spouse or for the pastor. Immediately stop those who want to use you in this way and insist that they go directly to the source.

- There may be times when individuals will quiz you as to how you feel about certain issues or actions of the board. It is inappropriate for you to discuss these issues.

Gary J. Blanchard
Assistant Superintendent
Illinois District Assemblies of God
Used with permission

POLICIES GOVERNING THE BOARD

The Board's Function

Appendices C through F contain policies that would be common to many churches. You may wish to ignore them and write your own policies that are completely different. However, you may want to begin with these as possible policies for your church. You could discuss each and delete those that don't apply and add others that do. You would also vary the wording to suit your unique ministry situation. I haven't included levels because they tend to confuse more than help in this type of document. Once the board has developed its policies, it would be wise to place them in a notebook for each board member to consult at the board meetings.

Job Description

The function of the board, on behalf of the congregation (if congregational rule), is to ensure the implementation of its primary and occasional responsibilities.

Primary Responsibilities

1. The board will pray for the congregation, the pastoral staff, and themselves.
2. The board will monitor (oversee) the church in several areas:
   - the church's spiritual condition
   - the church's direction (mission and vision)
   - the church's essential biblical doctrines
   - assuring that the church's beliefs agree with the essential doctrines of the Bible
   - assuring that the senior pastor agrees with the church's doctrinal statement and hires only staff that concur
   - assuring that those who teach agree with the doctrinal statement
   - the senior pastor's character and leadership, formally evaluating his ministry once a year
   - informally monitoring and addressing on a regular basis the pastor's performance and any questionable behavior
3. The board will make major decisions that affect the church. To facilitate its decision making, it will write church policy in at least three areas.
   - policies governing the board itself
   - policies governing the senior pastor
   - policies governing the board's relationship to the senior pastor
4. The board will serve in an advisory capacity to the senior pastor.

Occasional Responsibilities

1. The board will oversee the selection of the senior pastor.
2. The board will serve as an arbitrator in any disputes with the senior pastor.
3. The board will protect the senior pastor from those who would seek to undermine him or his ministry.
4. The board will ordain and license people for ministry.
   - The board will ordain those whom it feels God is leading into full-time ministry as a senior pastor or leadership staff in a church and who are qualified spiritually and have formal theological preparation.
   - The board will license those whom it feels God is leading into church or parachurch ministry and are spiritually qualified but may not have any theological preparation.

Board Members' Qualifications

Board members must meet the biblical and any other specified qualifications for board membership.

1. Board members should be reliable (trustworthy) and teachable persons (2 Tim. 2:2) who meet the spiritual leadership qualifications of 1 Timothy 3:1–7 and Titus 1:6–9.
2. They should have been in the church long enough to have proved themselves (1 Tim. 5:22), a minimum of two years.
3. They must agree with the church's core values, mission, vision, and strategy (this includes worship style).
4. They must agree with and fully support the church's doctrinal statement.
5. They need to be loyal to the lead pastor and his leadership but not to the point of rubber-stamping his agenda.
6. They should care about, respect, and trust one another, including the pastor (1 Tim. 3:2; 2 Tim. 2:2).
7. They should not be preservers of the status quo or tradition but open to new ways of doing ministry.
8. They should be members of the church who are involved in its ministry.
9. Their spouses must be supportive of their service on the board (for an example of what this might look like, see appendix B: The Role of a Board Member's Spouse).

Board Members' Conduct

The board commits itself and its members to ethical, biblical conduct, including proper use of authority and appropriate decorum when acting as board members.

1. Board members must work together as a unified team in the best interests of the entire church.
2. They must be courageous and make the right decisions no matter how unpopular or controversial.
3. They must trust and respect one another.
4. They must deal quickly and properly with any disagreements among themselves.
5. They must commit to regular attendance of board meetings.

6. They have no authority over others (other board members, senior pastor, staff, congregation) except when acting *corporately* as a board (see appendix J: The Church and Power).
7. When acting individually with the public, press, congregation, or others, they must not attempt to speak for the board, except to repeat explicitly stated board decisions.
8. They will not condone or voice criticism of the senior pastor or staff performance beyond the board, the senior pastor, or the staff person involved.
9. They will respect the confidentiality appropriate to issues of a sensitive nature.
10. They must avoid any conflict of interest with respect to their board positions.
    - Board members will not use their positions to obtain employment in the church for themselves, family members, or friends. Members desiring employment must resign from the board.
    - Members will disclose their involvements with other organizations or associations (such as fraternal organizations, other churches, parachurch ministries, etc.) that might pose a conflict of interest for the church.
11. They will enforce on themselves whatever discipline is needed to lead with excellence. Discipline will apply to matters such as attendance, preparation for meetings, conduct at meetings, policy-making principles, and respect of roles.

Note: For an example of how one organization has listed its code of conduct, see appendix I.

Board Operations

The board commits itself to operate biblically and efficiently as it conducts its meetings, making the best use of its time.

1. The board will make its decisions by consensus, defined as a simple majority vote. The final decision of any vote will be the position of the entire board (as if there were no difference of opinion).
2. The board will consist of seven people.
   - They will serve for three years and then rotate off for at least one year.
   - A new board member will be selected to serve out the term of one who resigns.

3. They will meet once a month to conduct business.
   - They will seek to do as much work as possible outside the board meetings.
   - They may elect to meet at other times to conduct business if necessary.
4. They will encourage differing viewpoints in striving for a spirit of unity.
5. They will focus on present and future issues rather than past issues.
6. They will operate proactively rather than passively or negatively.

Board Chairperson's Role

The board chairperson will assure the integrity and fulfillment of the board's process and, when necessary, may represent the board to the congregation and outside parties.

1. The job of the chairperson is to craft meeting agendas, guide orderly discussion, and see that the board conducts itself according to the policies that govern it.
2. The authority of the chairperson falls within the guidelines of board policy:
   - The chairperson will take the initiative in such matters as the following: determining meeting times and agenda items, recognizing board members and others who wish to address an issue, limiting discussion.
   - The chairperson as an individual has no authority to supervise or direct the other board members, including the senior pastor.
   - The chairperson does have the authority to interpret board policies for the board.
   - The chairperson will likely represent the board to the congregation and any outside persons in announcing board-stated positions. (However, the board will determine its spokesperson.)

Board Committees' Functions

Board committees, made up of people other than board members, will function solely to support the board's ministry as designated by the board.

1. Board committees function only to assist the board in accomplishing its ministry. (For example, they could assist the board by serving as a pulpit, finance, or building committee.)
2. They have no power. They cannot exercise authority over the board, senior pastor, his staff, or the congregation.
3. They will keep their business confidential, especially any issues of a private or sensitive nature.

Board Monitoring and Evaluation

The board will both monitor and evaluate its ministry performance for compliance with board policies.

1. The board will informally and regularly monitor its performance.
2. It will facilitate a formal, annual evaluation of its performance.
   • The board will individually and collectively evaluate its performance.
   • The senior pastor will conduct an informal evaluation of the board's performance.
   • The board will discuss these evaluations for the purpose of improving its leadership.
3. Its duties consist primarily of the policies that direct its ministry (Policies Governing the Board).

Board Members' Training

Because leaders are learners, the board will invest in and participate in its training on a regular basis.

1. All new board members will go through an orientation that informs them of the board's functions and the policies that govern the board, the senior pastor, and the board–senior pastor relationship.
2. All board members will have opportunity to add to their knowledge and hone their skills as members involved in the leadership process. (This could include such opportunities as reading books together, attendance at conferences and workshops, working with a church consultant, and other valuable training experiences.)

Choosing a Pastor

The board will follow biblical guidelines with respect to the qualifications of the senior pastor.

1. The board will seek a pastor who meets the character qualifications set forth in 1 Timothy 3:1–7 and Titus 1:6–9.
2. They will look for a pastor who has a good knowledge of Scripture and theology.
3. They will seek a pastor who has proven ministry competence.
   - He has proved to be a good communicator (preaching and teaching skills).
   - He has proved to be a good leader.
   - He has proved to be a strategic thinker.
4. They will pursue a pastor who essentially agrees with the church's core values, mission, vision, and strategy, including worship style.

Deciding on the Pastor's Compensation and Benefits

The board will pursue equity and fairness as well as follow biblical guidelines in establishing the senior pastor's compensation and benefits (1 Tim. 5:17–18).

1. The board will establish fair compensation (salary, housing, and utilities) and benefits (retirement, insurance, car allowance, etc.) according to the senior pastor's training, prior experience, size of the church, and tenure.
2. They will provide compensation that doesn't undermine the church's financial conditions.
3. They will determine any increases in the pastor's compensation and benefits based on the pastor's annual evaluation.

Note: This is a board policy on compensation and benefits rather than a board-approved wage and salary plan. However, the board may want to establish such a plan, possibly using a committee to do so.

Pastor's Emergency Succession

The board will protect the church from the sudden loss of the senior pastor's services by assigning at least one qualified person to lead in his place, such as an executive, associate, or assistant pastor, board chairperson, or another person who is reasonably familiar with the ministry.

APPENDIX *D*

POLICIES GOVERNING THE SENIOR PASTOR

The Senior Pastor's Function

Pastor's Job Description

The senior pastor will lead the congregation by protecting it from false doctrine, teaching and preaching the Scriptures, and by directing its activities (1 Tim. 5:17), including the supervision of all staff.

1. The senior pastor is to protect the congregation from false teaching (Acts 20:28).
2. The senior pastor will preach and teach the Bible (1 Tim. 5:17).
3. The senior pastor is to lead or direct the affairs of the church (1 Tim. 5:17).
   - pursues the church's mission and casts its vision (Matt. 28:19–20)
   - develops and implements the church's strategy
   - identifies the church's community for outreach
   - develops a disciple-making process
   - leads the church's staff

- assesses the church's location and facilities
- oversees the church's finances
- supervises all staff

4. The senior pastor (not the board) is ultimately responsible for the recruitment, hiring/enlistment, and dismissal of all paid and unpaid staff.
5. The senior pastor is ultimately responsible for the recruitment of paid and unpaid staff who agree with the church's core values, mission, vision, and strategy.
6. The senior pastor will encourage and provide opportunities for staff development.
7. The senior pastor will operate with written personnel policies that clarify personnel procedures for paid and volunteer staff.

Note: "Ultimately responsible" doesn't mean directly responsible. Other staff may hire people in their areas. However, final responsibility rests with the senior pastor.

Pastor's Board Responsibilities

The senior pastor will support the board and keep it informed about what is happening in the ministry.

1. The senior pastor will keep the board informed of any relevant trends, church issues, needs, external and internal changes, and problems that they should be aware of that are affecting or could affect the ministry positively or negatively.
2. The senior pastor will confront the board if he believes that it has violated its own governing policies and board-pastor policies in a way that is detrimental to their working relationship with him.
3. The senior pastor will provide the board with any information necessary for it to make fully informed decisions on the matters that come before it.

Pastor's Code of Conduct

1. The senior pastor will recognize the high visibility of his life and abstain from any appearance of evil (Rom. 14:1–23; 1 Tim. 3:1–7; Titus 1:7–9).
2. The senior pastor will make sure that conditions for paid and volunteer staff are fair and supportive of their ministries.

3. The senior pastor will not show preference toward nor discriminate against any staff member who properly expresses dissent.
4. The senior pastor will not prevent staff from grieving to the board when internal procedures have been exhausted.
5. The senior pastor will protect staff from those who might seek to undermine them or their ministries in some way.
   - The senior pastor will confront such people.
   - The senior pastor will initiate church discipline of those who persist.

Note: Rather than a board-approved personnel manual, there is board policy on the treatment of personnel. It's up to the senior pastor to decide on adopting a personnel manual.

Pastor's Financial Management

1. The senior pastor has the responsibility for oversight of the church's finances.
   - The board is responsible only to make policies governing financial management and the monitoring of the pastor's funds management.
   - The pastor is responsible for funds management.
   - The pastor will assign only approved personnel to handle the funds (for example, a treasurer or a business manager).
   - The pastor will oversee how those funds are handled (the collecting, counting, depositing, and accounting for all funds in a manner above reproach).
2. The senior pastor will lead in the development of a budget that plans for the expenditure of the church's finances.
   - This plan reflects projected income and expenditures.
   - This plan informs all church ministries of their funding for the coming year.
   - This plan will reflect the church's strategic planning (facilities expansion, disciple making, church planting, etc.).
3. The senior pastor is responsible to raise the funds necessary to meet the budget.
   - The pastor and others will regularly cast the church's vision.
   - The pastor and others will preach on and teach biblical principles of giving at least annually.
   - The pastor and others will invite its people publicly and privately to invest in God's kingdom.

- The pastor is responsible to see that the congregation is regularly informed of the church's financial condition.
4. The senior pastor will oversee the church's cash flow.
   - The pastor will monitor all income and expenses.
   - The pastor will communicate and account for all receipts and expenses to the board on a monthly basis.
   - The pastor may spend up to $_____ without board approval.
5. The senior pastor will manage staff compensation and benefits.
   - The pastor will establish a compensation and benefits package that fairly reflects the staff's academic training, prior experience, and ministry position in the church.
   - The pastor will establish a compensation and benefits package that is reasonable and affordable and is subject to the church's income.
   - The pastor may or may not automatically grant yearly cost of living increases.
   - The pastor will award bonuses based on each person's yearly accomplishment of ministry performance goals and responsibilities.

Pastor's Assets Management

The senior pastor will oversee the church's assets so that they are properly protected and well maintained.

1. The senior pastor is ultimately responsible to make sure that the church is insured against any casualty or theft losses and against any liability losses to board members, staff, or the congregation.
2. The senior pastor is ultimately responsible for the maintenance and repair of the church's facilities and equipment in a timely fashion.

Pastoral Committees

Pastoral committees, when used, will support the senior pastor's ministry and never interfere with his relationship with the board or staff.

1. Pastoral committees may be temporary or ongoing and exist to help the senior pastor accomplish his ministry as determined

by him. (Such committees might assist the pastor in strategic planning, budgeting, capital funds projects, facilities evaluation, preparing personnel manuals, conducting environmental scans, and so on.)

2. Pastoral committees may not speak or act for the senior pastor or staff except when given such authority for specific and time-limited purposes.

3. Pastoral committees have no power and will not exercise authority over the pastor or any of his staff.

Pastor's Retirement

Should the senior pastor retire, in deference to the new pastor, the retiring pastor will at his own initiative not remain at the church so as not to cause any potential problems such as divided loyalties on the part of the congregation or staff.

Pastor's Emergency Succession

The senior pastor will protect the church from the sudden loss of his services by recommending to the board and preparing at least one qualified person, who is reasonably familiar with his ministries, to lead in his place.

POLICIES GOVERNING THE BOARD-SENIOR PASTOR RELATIONSHIP

Pastor's Authority

The board corporately entrusts the senior pastor with the authority to be the primary leader of the church and its ministry.

1. The senior pastor answers to the board only when it acts corporately as the board.
2. The senior pastor as the primary, designated leader of the church has authority over individual board members except when they act corporately as the board.
   - The pastor may confront a board member over spiritual issues.
   - A board member will generally follow the leadership of the pastor when functioning on the board or serving in a church-related ministry.

- The pastor will not tell a board person how to decide an issue that the board is addressing corporately.
3. The senior pastor and all board members including the chairperson will minister together and relate to one another as equals.
4. The senior pastor does not answer to the board chairperson or any other individual board member, committee, or person(s) in the congregation.

Pastor's Accountability

The board will hold the senior pastor accountable and responsible for the church's paid and unpaid staff as well as their leadership.

1. The senior pastor has the board's invested authority over all paid and unpaid staff and their ministries, including the hiring or enlistment and the releasing of staff.
2. The senior pastor is responsible and accountable to the board for the staff and its ministry.
3. The board will not corporately or individually interfere with the staff in its ministry.
4. Individual board members when serving in staff-directed ministries will be under the direct authority of that staff person and the indirect authority of the pastor.

Pastor's Direction

The board will direct the senior pastor in his ministry through written policies that prescribe what he is and is not to accomplish, while allowing him some latitude in his interpretation of these policies.

1. The board will draft written policies that prescribe what the pastor may and may not do to accomplish the ministry's general direction (ends) and strategy (means).
   - The board will draft written policy that direct the pastor to accomplish biblically prescribed functions.
   - The board will draft written policies that determine what the pastor is not to attempt.
2. The board will design the policies so that they begin broadly and where necessary will be more specific in nature.

3. The board grants the pastor the latitude to interpret these policies within reason but retains the right to refine them further in areas of question or disagreement.
4. The board authorizes the pastor to draft all staff and congregational policies as he sees fit.

Pastor's Monitoring and Evaluation

The board will both monitor and evaluate the senior pastor's ministry performance.

1. The board will informally, regularly monitor the pastor's performance.
2. The board will facilitate a formal, annual evaluation of the pastor's performance.
   - The board will individually and collectively evaluate the senior pastor's performance.
   - The pastor will conduct a self-evaluation and a staff evaluation of his performance.

Pastor's Advising

The board will advise the senior pastor if he requests or seeks its advice. In this situation the pastor is free to choose whether or not he will take this advice.

MISSION STATEMENT
Ends Policies

Our mission is to move people at home and abroad from wherever they are spiritually (lost or saved) to become deeply mature believers in Christ. In order of priority, this involves the following four characteristics:

Converts

In moving people from prebirth to maturity, first, they must become converts of Christ.

1. Converts are people who have accepted Christ as Savior and are saved or born again.
2. Mature Christians are definitely converts.

Community

For converted people to become mature, they must experience community.

1. Converts in community are taught, encouraged, prayed for, and held accountable, among other things.
2. Mature people are in community (communal).

Commitment

In moving converts in community on to maturity, they must become deeply committed to Christ.

1. Converts in community have made the deepest commitment of their life to Christ.
2. Mature people are deeply committed people.

Contributors

In moving committed converts to maturity, they must become contributors to Christ's cause.

1. Contributors are the following kinds of people.
   - serving people (workers)
   - sharing people (witnesses)
   - supporting people (givers)
2. Mature people are contributors to Christ's cause.

Put your ends policies in a notebook for each board member to use at the board meetings, as it develops, applies, changes, and adds to them.

MEN'S CHARACTER ASSESSMENT FOR LEADERSHIP

Over the years, leaders have discovered that godly character is critical to effective ministry for Christ. However, no one is perfect, and all of us have our weaknesses and flaws as well as strengths. This character assessment is to help you determine your character strengths and weaknesses so that you can know where you are strong and where you need to develop and grow. The characteristics are found in 1 Timothy 3:1–7 and Titus 1:6–9.

Directions: Circle the number that best represents how you would rate yourself in each area.

1. I am "above reproach." I have a good reputation among people in general. I have done nothing that someone could use as an accusation against me.

   weak 1   2   3   4   5   6   7   8   strong

2. I am the "husband of one wife." If married, not only do I have one wife, but I am not physically or mentally promiscuous, for I am focused only on her.

   weak 1   2   3   4   5   6   7   8   strong

3. I am "temperate." I am a well-balanced person. I do not overdo anything, such as use of alcohol, TV watching, working, etc. I am not excessive or given to extremes in beliefs and commitments.

   weak 1   2   3   4   5   6   7   8   strong

4. I am "sensible." I show good judgment in life and have a proper perspective regarding myself and my abilities (I am humble).

   weak 1   2   3   4   5   6   7   8   strong

5. I am "respectable." I conduct my life in an honorable way, and people have and show respect for me.

   weak 1   2   3   4   5   6   7   8   strong

6. I am "hospitable." I use my residence as a place to serve and minister to Christians and non-Christians alike.

   weak 1   2   3   4   5   6   7   8   strong

7. I am "able to teach." When I teach the Bible, I show an aptitude for handling the Scriptures with reasonable skill.

   weak 1   2   3   4   5   6   7   8   strong

8. I am "not given to drunkenness." If I drink alcoholic beverages or indulge in other acceptable but potentially addictive practices, I do so in moderation.

   weak 1   2   3   4   5   6   7   8   strong

9. I am "not violent." I am under control. I do not lose control to the point that I strike other people or cause damage to their property.

   weak 1   2   3   4   5   6   7   8   strong

10. I am "gentle." I am a kind, meek (not weak), forbearing person. I do not insist on my rights or resort to violence.

   weak 1   2   3   4   5   6   7   8   strong

11. I am "not quarrelsome." I am a peacemaker who avoids hostile situations with people.

   weak 1   2   3   4   5   6   7   8   strong

12. I am "not a lover of money." I am not serving God for financial gain. I seek first his righteousness, knowing that God will supply my needs.

    weak   1   2   3   4   5   6   7   8   strong

13. I "manage my family well." If I have a family, my children are believers who obey me with respect. People do not think my children are wild or disobedient.

    weak   1   2   3   4   5   6   7   8   strong

14. I am "not a recent convert." I am not a new Christian who finds myself constantly struggling with pride and conceit.

    weak   1   2   3   4   5   6   7   8   strong

15. I have "a good reputation with outsiders." Though lost people may not agree with my religious convictions, they still respect me as a person.

    weak   1   2   3   4   5   6   7   8   strong

16. I am "not overbearing." I am not self-willed, stubborn, or arrogant.

    weak   1   2   3   4   5   6   7   8   strong

17. I am "not quick-tempered." I am not inclined toward anger and I do not lose my temper quickly and easily.

    weak   1   2   3   4   5   6   7   8   strong

18. I am "not pursuing dishonest gain." I am neither fond of nor involved in any wrongful practices that result in fraudulent gain.

    weak   1   2   3   4   5   6   7   8   strong

19. I "love what is good." I love the things that honor God.

    weak   1   2   3   4   5   6   7   8   strong

20. I am "upright." I live in accordance with the laws of God and man.

    weak   1   2   3   4   5   6   7   8   strong

21. I am "holy." I am a devout person whose life is generally pleasing to God.

    weak   1   2   3   4   5   6   7   8   strong

22. I "hold firmly to the faith." I understand, hold to, and attempt to conserve God's truth. I also encourage others while refuting those who oppose the truth.

> weak 1   2   3   4   5   6   7   8 strong

When you have completed this character assessment, note the characteristics to which you gave the lowest rating (a 4 or below). The lowest of these are to become the character goals that you work on to grow spiritually.

WOMEN'S CHARACTER ASSESSMENT FOR LEADERSHIP

Over the years, leaders have discovered that godly character is critical to effective ministry for Christ. However, no one is perfect, and all of us have our weaknesses and flaws as well as strengths. This character assessment is to help you determine your character strengths and weaknesses so that you can know where you are strong and where you need to develop and grow. The characteristics are found in 1 Timothy 2:9–10; 3:11; Titus 2:3–5; and 1 Peter 3:1–4.

Directions: Circle the number that best represents how you would rate yourself in each area.

1. I am "worthy of respect." I find that most people who know me respect me and tend to honor me as a dignified person who is serious about spiritual things.

   weak 1   2   3   4   5   6   7   8 strong

2. I am not a "malicious talker." I do not slander people whether believers or unbelievers.

   weak 1   2   3   4   5   6   7   8 strong

3. I am "temperate." I am a well-balanced person. I do not overdo any activity, such as use of alcohol, TV watching, working, etc. I am not excessive or given to extremes in beliefs and commitments.

   weak   1   2   3   4   5   6   7   8   strong

4. I am "trustworthy in everything." The Lord and people find me to be a faithful person in everything I do.

   weak   1   2   3   4   5   6   7   8   strong

5. I live "reverently." I have a deep respect for God and live in awe of him.

   weak   1   2   3   4   5   6   7   8   strong

6. I am "not addicted to much wine." If I drink alcoholic beverages, I do so in moderation. I am not addicted to them.

   weak   1   2   3   4   5   6   7   8   strong

7. I teach "what is good." I share with other women what God has taught me from his Word and life in general.

   weak   1   2   3   4   5   6   7   8   strong

8. I "love my husband." If I am married, I love my husband according to 1 Corinthians 13:4–8.

   weak   1   2   3   4   5   6   7   8   strong

9. I "love my children." If I have children, I love my children and care for them.

   weak   1   2   3   4   5   6   7   8   strong

10. I am "self-controlled." I do not let other people or things run my life, and I do what I know to be right.

    weak   1   2   3   4   5   6   7   8   strong

11. I am "pure." I am not involved emotionally or physically in sexual immorality.

    weak   1   2   3   4   5   6   7   8   strong

12. I am "busy at home." If I am married, I take care of my responsibilities at home.

    weak   1   2   3   4   5   6   7   8   strong

13. I am "kind." I am essentially a good person.

    weak   1   2   3   4   5   6   7   8   strong

14. I am "subject to my husband." If I am married, I let my husband take responsibility for and lead our marriage, and I follow his leadership.

    weak   1   2   3   4   5   6   7   8   strong

15. I have "a gentle and quiet spirit." I am a mild, easygoing person who wins people over by a pure and reverent life more than by my words.

    weak   1   2   3   4   5   6   7   8   strong

16. I "dress modestly." I wear clothing that is decent and shows propriety.

    weak   1   2   3   4   5   6   7   8   strong

17. I "do good deeds." I do those things that are appropriate for women who profess to know and worship God.

    weak   1   2   3   4   5   6   7   8   strong

When you have completed this character assessment, note those characteristics that you gave the lowest rating (a 4 or below). The lowest of these are to become the character goals that you work on to grow spiritually.

BOARD MEMBER COVENANT

The following is a board member covenant developed for the Assemblies of God Church.

- *Attendance.* Every board member is expected to maintain consistent and regular attendance. Board members are to be present for Sunday school, Sunday morning and evening worship services, and Wednesday evening services. Board members are expected to attend all board meetings.
- *Stewardship.* Board members are expected to be faithful stewards. They are to be responsible in the way they conduct their personal business and financial affairs. Board members must support the ministry of the church through their tithe.
- *Ministry.* Being a board member is not a passive position. Board members are expected to be actively involved in the ministries of the church. They are to be an extension of the pastor's ministry to the congregation.
- *Training.* Learning is a lifelong process. Board members are expected to continue to learn how to better serve the church.
- *Example.* Board members must set the example for the church family. Their lifestyle must be free of addictive drugs, alcoholic

beverages, and sinful habits. Their marriage must be strong and free from activities that might be construed as unholy.

- *Doctrine.* All board members will faithfully support the doctrines of the Assemblies of God.
- *Confidentiality.* Board members will keep matters confidential.
- *Prayer.* Board members will faithfully pray for the pastor, the church, and for those in leadership.

Gary J. Blanchard
Assistant Superintendent
Illinois District Assemblies of God
Reprinted with permission

THE CHURCH AND POWER
Individual and Corporate Power

Church leadership boards as well as others in the church must be aware of individual and corporate power and the roles that each plays in church leadership. The implications of these will be seen in the section below on two scenarios for handling power.

Individual power is power that is held by an individual in the ministry. (It could be personal or position power.) The individual exercises that power when leading others. For example, the senior pastor exercises individual power as the designated leader of the church. Some other leader in the church has individual power to lead his or her ministry within the church (Heb. 13:17). A negative example is when some person, such as a board member or congregant, attempts to exercise individual authority over the senior pastor.

Corporate power is exercised by a group, such as a church board or an entire congregation. When a board makes a decision corporately or a congregation votes on some issue as a whole, they're exercising their corporate authority. This kind of power usually has precedence over individual power. Thus a board acting corporately would have power over a senior pastor. A congregation acting corporately would have authority over a governing board in a congregationally ruled church.

The Church's Relationship to Power

Power resides in every church whether it wants it or not. The important question is how the church, whether universal or local, should handle its power as it seeks to influence people for God. The answer is church polity. Polity concerns whom the church empowers. It answers the question, Who has the authority to exercise power in the church? No less than three major types of polity or government have surfaced over the years—episcopal, presbyterian, and congregational.

The Bishops Have the Power

The episcopal form of polity or government is hierarchical. It places the power to influence in the hands of bishops. Churches that practice this form of government follow a threefold ministry hierarchy, which includes bishops, presbyters, and deacons. Only the bishops have the power to consecrate other bishops and ordain priests and deacons. Thus the bishops hold the power in this system. Some people attempt to trace this authority back to the apostles (apostolic succession).

There is biblical support for presbyters or elders as well as deacons (1 Tim. 3:1–10 and other passages); however, the office of bishop appears to be the same as the office of elder, as we saw in chapter 4, not a separate office with superior power over the others. Consequently, the episcopal form has little biblical support. This polity is practiced primarily by the Methodist, Orthodox, Anglican, Episcopal, and Roman Catholic churches.

The Elders Have the Power

The presbyterian form of polity is federal—it places the power to influence in the hands of certain leaders, often called elders. A number of churches that practice this polity are governed by a session that is composed of two kinds of elders. One is the ruling elders. They're laypeople who are elected by the congregation. They assist in the government of the church. The other is a teaching elder. This person is the pastor or minister who is ordained by other ministers. The teaching elder is responsible to minister the Word and sacraments to the church. Other churches have variations of this format, such as a board of lay elders with one elder who serves as a teaching elder.

There is ample scriptural support for this form of government. Elders are involved as leaders throughout the New Testament (Acts 11:30; 14:23; 15:2, 22; 20:17; Titus 1:5; James 5:14; and 1 Peter 5:1). In 1 Timothy 5:17, Paul refers to the elders at Ephesus who "direct the affairs of the church." They are worthy of double honor, especially those who also teach and preach. Apparently some ruled, and others ruled and also taught. However, as we saw in chapter 4, this is likely a reference to the city church made up of these elders who were likely the pastors of house churches located all over Ephesus. Some would use 1 Thessalonians 5:12–13 and Hebrews 13:17 to argue that congregants should submit to the elders. These two passages may be referring to elders, but they don't identify the leaders as such.

This polity is practiced primarily by Presbyterian and Reformed groups, as well as by some independent and Bible churches. Most hold that both classes of elders are of equal ministries and have equal authority in the church.

The Congregation Has the Power

The congregational form of polity gives power to the congregation to exercise influence over its affairs. Churches that practice this polity emphasize that the church is to be a democratic community that vests ultimate authority in the membership or congregation. They acknowledge Christ as head of the church. They often elect ministers to lead them who theoretically have no more power than any other member of the congregation. They also elect boards (elder, deacon, and other) to lead and conduct much of the church's business.

A primary argument for a congregational polity is the priesthood of the believer (1 Peter 2:5, 9). Another argument uses the passages that imply that congregations made decisions in certain situations (see Acts 6:3, 5; 15:22; 2 Cor. 8:19). The congregation's involvement in church discipline (see Matt. 18:17; 1 Cor. 5:4–5) is another argument for congregational polity.

This polity is practiced by Baptists and numerous other denominational and independent churches.

Who Should Have the Power?

The logical question to ask next is, Which form of polity is the biblically correct view? However, it would be better to ask if there is a specific, biblically correct form. The congregational and presbyterian forms appear to have the most biblical support. The question comes down to whether Scripture prescribes one form over the other. As we saw above, both positions appeal to specific passages of Scripture that seem to validate their particular form. However, Ryrie accurately observes that, "The New Testament picture seems to include a blend of congregational and federal government, limited to the local level."[1]

This would seem to indicate that Scripture doesn't validate a particular polity. Apparently, the early churches embraced various structures within the federal and congregational forms for handling power that conformed best to their unique circumstances. That is likely why we see a blending of the two forms. Thus it would appear that churches today are free to choose their polity, as long as it conforms to clear prescriptive passages and doesn't violate Scripture. In short, Scripture leaves it up to each church to determine its own structures for handling power and authority. Consequently, each church is free to determine how it will structure itself to deal with power and its potential abuse.

Two Guiding Biblical Principles

In addition to the passages above regarding the federal and congregational views, there are some other biblical principles that can help churches structure themselves as they attempt to handle their power. Scripture prescribes that people obey their leaders. In Hebrews 13:17 the writer says to the people: "Obey your leaders and submit to their authority. . . . Obey them so that their work will be a joy, not a burden, for that would be of no advantage to you." This passage is clear that the leaders in the church, whether elders or others, have authority and that followers are to obey them as leaders with authority.

Another principle is that it's wise to pursue the counsel of others. In several places, Proverbs encourages believers to seek the advice of several people, because there is wisdom in learning the viewpoints of others (Prov. 11:14; 15:22; 20:18; 24:6). The point is that all of us are wiser than one of us. Thus I would argue that churches would be wise to have good, godly, competent governing boards. I'll say more about this below.

Two Scenarios for Handling Power

The federal and congregational views, or a combination, have the most biblical support and, at least in the West, represent the polity of most churches. The following presents two scenarios for the distribution of power in each. The advantage of both is that they clearly spell out the lines of authority between the board, the pastor, and the congregation as well as achieve a reasonable balance of power.

THE CONGREGATIONAL SCENARIO

The congregational scenario places much of the power in the hands of the congregation. However, the congregation may only exercise that power corporately, such as when it comes together to vote on some issue. The congregation might vote on the board members and pastor once a year. No individual congregant has individual power over anyone else, including the senior pastor and staff.

The board has corporate power to act on behalf of the congregation. If the congregation doesn't agree with the board's decisions, it can vote out all or some of the board members at its next official meeting. Regardless, no board member has individual power over anyone else. (An exception is when he or she is leading a ministry within the church. Then he or she would have some individual authority over those in that ministry—Heb. 13:17.)

The senior pastor is a board member with one vote that he exercises when the board acts corporately. He also has individual power over board members, staff, and individual congregants as the congregation's recognized leader (Heb. 13:7, 17). Other leaders in the church would have some individual authority over those who minister under them. However, neither the pastor nor other leaders have individual power over the congregation as a whole.

THE FEDERAL SCENARIO

The federal scenario places much of the power in the hands of the board that selects its own members, not in the congregation. The idea is that the most spiritual, godly leaders in the church serve on this board. However, they may only exercise their power corporately as a board. No board member may exercise individual power over the senior pastor or staff. (They may have individual authority over congregants that are part of a ministry they might lead.)

The pastor should be on the board but has only one vote like any other board member when making corporate decisions. However, as the senior pastor and leader of the church, he has individual power over individual board members, the staff, and the congregation (Heb. 13:7, 17).

The congregation has no corporate or individual power. While it may have many godly members, it also has those who are uncommitted, carnal, and possibly some unsaved people who shouldn't be involved in making decisions that affect the spiritual vitality and future of the church. This scenario has the most biblical support.

SKILLMAN BIBLE CHURCH GOVERNANCE POLICY

S killman Bible Church is a congregation of fewer than one hundred people, located in Dallas, Texas. Following are the policies that its board drafted.

In April of 2002 the board began a study of policy governance to better define its role as the board for Skillman Bible Church. They elected to utilize the Carver series of twelve studies on policy governance,[1] which would take approximately nine to twelve months to study. They also viewed a video by John Carver[2] and made available other resources to board members for independent study. The goal was to form a policy governance statement for the church, both for the present and the future. It would define (1) the purpose of the board, (2) the role of the board, and (3) the roles of the members of the board.

Additionally the board was interested in better defining its relationship to the pastor of the church. They compiled notes of the study, appending them as the study continued throughout the year. This document is the summary of those notes and presents the conclusions that were reached. It has resulted in the first statement of policy governance for Skillman Bible Church. The Carver series will continue to be on file in the church library should any future board member, or member of the church, wish to study the subject. Books 1 and 2 especially will be important for understanding the overview. It goes without saying that this document concentrates on the philosophical and practical aspects of governing, and the high quality biblical leadership and character traits, by which the leaders at Skillman Bible Church are chosen, are assumed.

I. Basic Principles of Policy Governance
   a. The primary role of the board at Skillman Bible Church is to provide written policy on the intended "ends" (purpose, vision, mission, and goals), which will empower the staff, leaders, and members of SBC to perform ministry to our community and our world.
   b. An additional role of the board is to establish clear limitations on the execution of such ministry, which will bring about those ends.
   c. The board will also clarify the roles of the board, which directs the organization of the church (and who are leaders within the congregation as elders and deacons), and the senior pastor who will lead the entire congregation in ministry toward the ends within the limits set by the board.

II. Roles and Responsibilities of Board Members
   a. The board is chosen by the church as "trustees" to govern well on behalf of the members, the community, the world, and the Lord.
   b. While the board seeks—even demands—diversity, when it speaks, it speaks as one voice.
   c. The board members are committed to faithful attendance and study of board issues in order to be prepared at meetings.
   d. The design of the board is important; we cannot simply expect to overcome bad design with good people.
   e. Some things the board cannot delegate: linkage to the member of the church, policy making responsibility, and executive evaluation.
   f. At SBC board members must learn to wear different hats. Their responsibility as a board member is different from the role as an elder or deacon. And responsibility as member of the church is different from roles as elders, deacons, or board members. Difficult, but important, is remembering that we don't bring those hats to the boardroom. Or at least we wear them differently.
   g. Board members will take a "hands-off" approach to approving programs, determining staffing needs, and designing minis-

tries—even budgeting. Those are ministry jobs, which board members may have individually while wearing another hat. But strictly speaking they are not board jobs.

h. The basic board job is to determine fence posts for the pastures, rules for the playing fields of ministry. How the ministry gets done is up to the staff.

i. Our most important approaches[3] to the board jobs are (1) be prepared to participate responsibly, (2) honor divergent opinion without being intimidated, (3) support the board's final choice, and (4) don't tolerate putting off big issues.

III. The Chairman's Role on the Board

a. The chairman, chosen annually by peers, bears a heavy responsibility with respect to good governance.

b. Intentional direction and discipline are important so that the next chairman knows where we left off.

c. Good written records are essential to see that the board moves forward. We choose a secretary from peers to record the process. He works with the chair to accurately record and distribute documents.

d. The chairman must understand governance process, and how a group of peers can be visionary, bold, and pragmatic all at the same time.

e. The job is as much about nurturance as cracking the whip, as much about thorough deliberation as about decisiveness, and as much about stimulating diversity as about reaching a single, official decision. The job is to encourage, cajole, pressure, and cheerlead.

IV. Board Meetings

a. Meetings are not for details. We work on the details outside of meetings. Instead the focus primarily is on orderly long-range vision and boundaries.

b. Meetings are for group study and decision.

c. Meetings are for writing policy, actually for approving policy that is usually worked on outside meetings. We may hear ministry reports but only in summarized form to maintain our link with the ministry and members.

d. For the most part we meet only monthly and not late. We may have focused retreat times during the year to expand efforts on vision.

e. Staff and ministry decisions should generally not be on the agenda.

f. The board will make its own agenda for meetings. The chair only organizes and directs it. The board agenda is crucial.[4] It should at least (1) maintain an up-to-date job description, (2) express the job description in outcomes, (3) review desired board and staff performance objectives annually, and (4) adopt the board schedule for the year.

V. Creating a Mission That Makes a Difference[5]

   a. Our mission statement should be addressing the following: How are we different from the church down the street? We should be continually evaluating and improving our statement.

   b. The statement must be careful on how we use verbs. We want to use "ends" verbs and not "means" verbs.

   c. One focus we have is building up leaders and missionaries to send them out. This needs to be included in the statement.

   d. Another question answered by our statement is "How will the world be different because of our church?"

   e. Finally, we need to be working with other churches and ministries in this effort of defining mission and working together.

VI. Board Assessment of the Pastor

   a. A role of the board is to assess the performance of the pastor, our executive head. The board will do so by evaluating primarily whether or not the church is completing the stated mission of the board effectively.

   b. All ministries in the church are accountable to the pastor.

   c. If the board hasn't established how it should be, it won't ask how it is. Any expectations the board has of the pastor will be in writing. The board will be careful to distinguish between espoused values and held values.

VII. Board Self-Assessment

   a. Policy making is an ongoing process. So the board will be constantly evaluating values and policies.

   b. The board will evaluate often whether we are overstepping bounds into directing ministry. It must keep focused into setting vision and establishing boundaries.

   c. The board must make certain it keeps a strong linkage with the members to ensure the church is carrying out the vision.

   d. The board members will hold each other accountable to do the task of the board.[6] They must create an environment through productive linkage, between members and board, to enable unpaid and paid staff to organize effective ministry to meet the church's ends—making new and stronger believers. They will also have written governing policies that broadly address ends, executive limitations, governing processes, and board staff linkage. And they will encourage and evaluate executive pastoral performance.

VIII. Financial and Other Matters

a. While it is the board's responsibility to assure the church is fiscally sound, the staff will prepare and oversee the budget under the direction of the pastor. Regular reporting shall monitor the financial status of the church.

b. It is the purpose of the board to get beyond the numbers to the ends of the church's mission. Budgeting by staff shall not deviate from the board's ends priorities or fail to show acceptable foresight. The staff should not allow reporting that (1) contains too little information for accurate projections, (2) plans operational expenditures in any year that exceeds conservatively projected revenue, or (3) does not incorporate at least three years of overall planning.[7]

Used by permission

LAKE POINTE CHURCH POLICIES

L ake Pointe Church is where I attend. It's a megachurch of around seven thousand people who meet in Rockwall, Texas, a suburb of Dallas.

Policies Governing the Board (The Board's Function)

Board Job Description

The purpose of the board, on behalf of the congregation, is to see to it that the church (1) achieves its mission and (2) observes biblical standards. The specific job of the board is to ensure the implementation of its primary and occasional responsibilities, which include but are not limited to the following:

PRIMARY RESPONSIBILITIES

1. The board will pray for the congregation, the pastoral staff, and themselves.
2. The board will oversee the church's spiritual condition.

3. The board will produce and authorize overall written church policy in four areas.
   a. The policies governing the board itself.
   b. The policies governing the senior pastor.
   c. The policies governing the board's relationship to the senior pastor.
   d. The policies reflecting the church's theology and practices.
4. The board will provide supervision of, accountability for, and protection of the senior pastor.
5. The board is responsible for church discipline.
6. The board is responsible for doctrinal clarification.
7. The board is responsible for approving the licensing and ordination of individuals to the gospel ministry.

OCCASIONAL RESPONSIBILITIES

8. The board will oversee the selection process of the senior pastor.
9. The board will serve as an arbitrator in any disputes with the senior pastor.
10. The board will enforce policy relative to board members' attendance, preparation, policy-making principles, respect of roles, and ensuring continuance of leadership capability.
11. The board will continually work on its development, including orientation of new board members in the board's governance process, periodic discussion of process improvement, and continuous education of board members.
12. The board is responsible for establishing fair compensation and benefits for the senior pastor according to his training, prior experience, size of church, tenure, and productivity.

Leadership Style

The board will lead with an emphasis on strategically accomplishing the church's stated purpose, including (1) evangelism and discipleship, (2) encouragement of different viewpoints, (3) leadership rather than administrative detail, (4) clear distinction of board and senior pastor roles, (5) collective rather than individual decisions, (6) future focus rather than past or present, and (7) proactivity rather than reactivity, passivity, or negativity.

Chairperson's Role

The board's chairperson will assure the integrity and fulfillment of the board's process and, when necessary, may represent the board to the congregation and to outside parties. The job of the chairperson is to see that the board behaves consistently within its own rules and those legitimately imposed upon it from outside the organization. Accordingly:

1. Deliberation will be fair, open, and thorough but also timely, orderly, and to the point.
2. The chairperson is empowered to chair board meetings with all the commonly accepted power of that position (for example, ruling, recognizing).
3. The chairperson may represent the board to outside parties in announcing board-stated positions and in stating chair decisions and interpretations within the area delegated to him.
4. In such cases where the chairperson is not the senior pastor, the chairperson has no authority to supervise and direct the senior pastor.

Board Members' Qualifications

Board members must meet the biblical and other prudent qualifications for board membership (1 Tim. 3:1–7; 1 Tim. 5:22; 2 Tim. 2:2; Titus 1:5–9).

1. Board members should be reliable (trustworthy) and teachable men who must meet spiritual leadership qualifications.
2. They should have sufficient tenure in the church to have proven themselves to be fully developing followers of Christ.
3. They need to agree with the church's core values, mission, vision, strategy, and doctrine.
4. Though they're not to be yes men, they do need to be loyal to the senior pastor and his leadership.
5. They must be members who are involved in the ministry of the church.
6. Their spouses must be supportive of their service on the board.

Board Members' Code of Conduct

The board commits itself and its members to ethical, biblical conduct, including proper use of authority and appropriate decorum when acting as board members.

Accordingly:

1. Board members must work together as a unified team in the best interests of the entire church.

2. They must be courageous and make the right decisions no matter how unpopular or controversial.
3. They must trust and respect one another.
4. They must deal well with disagreements among themselves.
5. They must care about, genuinely appreciate, and most importantly respect and trust one another (this includes the senior pastor).
6. They must not be preservers of the status quo or tradition but open to new ways of doing ministry.
7. They must commit to attend the meetings of the board.
8. They may not attempt to exercise individual authority over the organization except as explicitly set forth in board policies.
   a. Board members have authority over others (other board members, senior pastor, staff, congregation) only when acting *corporately* as a board.
   b. They must not attempt to exercise *individual* authority over others in the church (other board members, senior pastor, staff, congregation).
9. Their individual interaction with the public, press, congregation, or others must not attempt to speak for the board except to repeat explicitly stated board decisions.
10. They will not condone or voice criticism of the senior pastor or staff performance beyond the board, the senior pastor, or the staff person involved.
11. They will respect the confidentiality appropriate to issues of a sensitive nature.
12. They must avoid conflict of interest with respect to their board member responsibilities.
13. They will not corporately or individually interfere with the staff in its ministry.
14. Members, when serving in staff-directed ministries, will be under the direct authority of that staff person and the indirect authority of the pastor.

Board Member's Operations

The board commits itself to operate biblically and efficiently in conducting its meetings, making the best use of its time. Accordingly:

1. The board will make its decisions by consensus, defined as a simple majority vote. The final decision will be the position of the board (as if there were no difference of opinion).
2. The election and term of board members should comply with the church's bylaws and constitution.

Evaluation of Board Members

On an annual basis, the board will evaluate itself in written form corporately. Additionally, each board member will conduct a self-evaluation.

Policies Governing the Senior Pastor (The Senior Pastor's Function)

Pastor's Job Description

The senior pastor oversees the general spiritual condition of the church and leads its operational ministry, including all staff.

1. The senior pastor is to protect the congregation from false teaching (Acts 20:28).
2. The senior pastor will preach and teach the Bible (1 Tim. 5:17).
3. The senior pastor is to lead or direct the affairs of the church (1 Tim. 5:17).
   - Pursues the church's mission and casts its vision (Matt. 28:19–20)
   - Develops and implements the church's strategy
   - Identifies the church's community for outreach
   - Develops a disciple-making process
   - Leads the church's staff
   - Assesses the church's location and facilities
   - Oversees the church's finances
   - Establishes culturally relevant evangelistic ministries to reach lost people
   - Establishes edifying ministries that move saved people toward spiritual maturity as well as address their spiritual needs
4. The senior pastor (not the board) is ultimately responsible for the recruitment, hiring/enlistment, and dismissal of all paid and unpaid staff.
5. The senior pastor is ultimately responsible for the recruitment of paid and unpaid staff that agree with the church's core values, mission, vision, and strategy.
6. The senior pastor will encourage and provide opportunities for staff development.
7. The senior pastor will operate within applicable personnel policies that clarify personnel procedures for paid and volunteer staff.

Note: "Ultimately responsible" does not mean directly responsible. Other staff may hire people in their areas. However, final responsibility rests with the senior pastor (the "buck stops" with him).

Pastor's Board Responsibilities

The senior pastor will support and keep the board informed in its ministry.

1. The senior pastor will keep the board informed of any relevant trends, church issues, needs, external and internal changes, and problems that they should be aware of that are affecting or could affect the ministry positively or negatively.
2. The senior pastor will confront the board if he believes that it has violated its own governing policies and board-pastor policies in a way that is detrimental to its working relationship with him.
3. The senior pastor will provide the board with any information necessary for it to make fully informed decisions on the matters that come before it.

Pastor's Code of Conduct

1. The senior pastor is responsible to see that the church's ministries address the spiritual needs of its members and attenders.
2. The senior pastor will recognize the high visibility of his life and abstain from even the appearance of evil (1 Tim. 3:1–7; Titus 1:7–9; Rom. 14:1–23).
3. The senior pastor shall make sure that conditions for paid and volunteer staff are fair and supportive of their ministries.
4. The senior pastor will not show preference toward nor discriminate against any staff member who properly expresses dissent.
5. The senior pastor will not prevent staff from grieving to the board when internal procedures have been exhausted.
6. The senior pastor will protect staff from those who might seek to undermine them or their ministries in some way.
   - The senior pastor will confront such people.
   - The senior pastor will initiate church discipline of those that persist.

Note: Rather than a board-approved personnel manual, there is board policy on the treatment of personnel.

Pastor's Financial Management

1. The senior pastor has the responsibility for oversight of the church's finances.
   - The board is responsible only to make policies governing financial management and the monitoring of the pastor's funds management.
   - The pastor is responsible for funds management.
   - The pastor will assign only approved personnel to handle the funds (a treasurer, a business manager, etc.).
   - The pastor will oversee how those funds are handled (the collecting, counting, depositing, and accounting for all funds in a manner that is above reproach).
2. The senior pastor will lead the staff to create a budget for church approval that plans for the expenditure of the church's finances.
   - This plan reflects projected income and expenditures.
   - This plan informs all church ministries of their funding for the coming year.
   - This plan will reflect the church's strategic planning (facilities expansion, disciple making, church planting, etc.).
3. The senior pastor is responsible to raise the funds necessary to meet the budget.
   - The pastor and others will regularly cast the church's vision.
   - The pastor and others will preach on and teach biblical principles of giving at least on an annual basis.
   - The pastor and others will invite the people of Lake Pointe publicly and privately to invest in God's kingdom.
   - The pastor is responsible to see that the congregation is regularly informed of the church's financial condition.
4. The senior pastor will oversee the church's cash flow.
   - The pastor will monitor all income and expenses.
   - The pastor will communicate and account for all receipts and expenses to the board on a monthly basis.
   - Nonbudgeted expenditures by the pastor should be reported to the board within thirty days. Nonbudgeted expenditures of over $20,000 should have prior board approval.
5. The senior pastor will manage staff compensation and benefits.
   - The pastor will establish a compensation and benefits package that fairly reflects the staff's abilities, prior experience, and ministry position in the church.

- The pastor will establish a compensation and benefits package that is reasonable and affordable and is subject to the church's income.
- The pastor may or may not automatically grant yearly cost of living increases.
- The pastor may award bonuses and merit increases based on each person's yearly accomplishment of ministry performance goals and responsibilities.

Pastor's Asset Management

The senior pastor will oversee the church's assets so that they are properly protected and well maintained.

1. The senior pastor is ultimately responsible to make sure that the church is insured against any casualty or theft losses and against any liability losses to board members, staff, or the congregation.
2. The senior pastor is ultimately responsible for the maintenance and repair of the church's facilities and equipment in a timely fashion.

Pastoral Committees

Pastoral committees, when used, will support the senior pastor's ministry and never interfere with his relationship with the board or staff.

1. Pastoral committees may be temporary or ongoing and exist to help the senior pastor accomplish his ministry as determined by him. (Such committees might assist the pastor in strategic planning, budgeting, facilities evaluation, preparing personnel manuals, conducting environmental scans, and so on.)
2. Pastoral committees may not speak or act for the senior pastor or staff except when given such authority for specific and time-limited purposes.
3. Pastoral committees have no power and will not exercise authority over the pastor or any of his staff.

Pastor's Emergency Succession

The senior pastor will protect the church from the sudden loss of his services by recommending to the board and preparing at least one qualified person to lead in his place who is reasonably familiar with his duties.

Policies Governing the Board–Senior Pastor Relationship (The Board's Relationship with the Senior Pastor)

Pastor's Authority

The board corporately entrusts the senior pastor with the authority to be the primary leader of the church and its ministry.

1. The senior pastor answers only to the board when it acts corporately as the board.
2. The senior pastor as the primary, designated leader of the church has authority over individual board members except when they act corporately as the board.
   - The pastor may confront a board member over spiritual issues.
   - A board member will generally follow the leadership of the pastor when functioning on the board or serving in a church-related ministry.
   - The pastor will not tell a board person how to decide an issue that the board is addressing corporately.
3. The senior pastor and all board members including the chairman will minister together and relate to one another as if they are equals.
4. The senior pastor is not under the authority of the board chairman, any individual board member, any other board committee, or any individual in the congregation.

Pastor's Accountability

The board will hold the senior pastor accountable and responsible for his performance as well as for the performance of the church's paid and unpaid staff.

Pastor's Supervision

The board will supervise the senior pastor.

1. The board will draft written policies as needed that prescribe what the pastor may and may not do to accomplish the ministry's general direction (ends) and strategy (means). Additionally, as needed, the board will draft written policies that direct the pastor to accomplish biblically prescribed functions.
2. The board will design the policies so that they begin broadly and, where necessary, will be more specific in nature.

3. The board grants the pastor the latitude to interpret these policies within reason but retains the right to refine them further in areas of question or disagreement.
4. The board authorizes the pastor to draft all staff policies as he sees fit.

Pastor's Monitoring and Evaluation

The board will both monitor and evaluate the senior pastor's ministry performance.

1. The board will informally, regularly monitor the pastor's performance.
2. The board will facilitate a formal, annual evaluation of the pastor's performance.
   - The board will collectively evaluate the senior pastor's performance.
   - The senior pastor will conduct a self-evaluation and will receive an evaluation from his direct reports.

Used by permission

BOARD POLICIES
Lancaster County Bible Church

L ancaster County Bible Church is a large church located at 2392 Mount Joy Road in Manheim, Pennsylvania.

Policy of the Board of Elders

Staff Limitations
Global Staff Constraint
Policy Serial Number: SL #1
Date of Adoption: 15 Dec. 2003

The senior pastor shall not cause or allow any practice, activity, decision, or organizational circumstance that is either unbiblical, unlawful, imprudent, in violation of the LCBC Constitution and Bylaws, or commonly accepted business and professional ethics and practices.

Policy of the Board of Elders

Staff Limitations
Treatment of Attendees
Policy Serial Number: SL #2a
Date of Adoption: 15 Dec. 2003

With respect to interactions with LCBC attendees, the senior pastor shall not cause or allow conditions, procedures, or decisions that are unsafe, undignified, or unnecessarily intrusive. No person or class of persons shall be restricted from attending or be made to feel unwelcome at any public event of the church, except to address disruptive behavior or in cases explicitly determined by the elder board.

Further, without limiting the scope of the foregoing by this enumeration, he shall not:

1. Fail to maintain an environment that discourages behavior that is sinful, unsafe, or abusive.
   a. Fail to approach discipline and conflict resolution matters in a spirit of gentleness and humility (Gal. 6:1–2) and without bias or partiality (1 Tim. 5:21).
   b. Fail to ensure due process through the creation of a comprehensive procedure in discipline and conflict resolution matters as commanded in the New Testament (Matt. 18:15–20).
   c. Fail to pursue discipline and conflict resolution situations until repentance or resolution is achieved or inform the elder board when due process has been exhausted at the staff level.
2. Fail to ensure clear understanding among all attendees of the purpose, scope, and expectations of LCBC ministry entities.
3. Fail to operate facilities with appropriate accessibility and privacy.
4. Use methods of collecting, reviewing, transmitting, or storing attendee information that fail to protect against improper access to or use of the material elicited.
5. Elicit information for which there is no clear necessity.
6. Use methods for fund-raising or recruitment of volunteers that would cause widespread resentment.

Policy of the Board of Elders

Staff Limitations
Treatment of Staff
Policy Serial Number: SL #2b
Date of Adoption: 15 Dec. 2003

With respect to the treatment of paid and volunteer staff, the senior pastor shall not cause or allow conditions that are unfair, undignified, disorganized, or unclear.

Further, without limiting the scope of the foregoing by this enumeration, he shall not:

1. Operate without written personnel rules that: (a) state expectations for staff, (b) provide for effective handling of grievances, and (c) protect against wrongful conditions.
2. Fail to ensure that staff are adequately qualified, trained, and monitored within their scope of responsibility.
3. Fail to ensure among staff a clear understanding of the purpose, scope, and expectations of LCBC ministry entities.
4. Permit outside employment opportunities of paid staff to: (a) interfere with the scope of responsibility, (b) cause any perceived or real conflict(s) of interest, or (c) create undue stress on co-workers.
   a. Fail to seek board approval for any recurring or continuing outside employment opportunity offered to or sought by the senior pastor.
5. Allow staff to be unprepared to deal with emergency situations or media coverage.
6. Fail to acquaint staff with the senior pastor's interpretation of their protections under this policy.

Policy of the Board of Elders

Staff Limitations
Financial Planning/Budgeting
Policy Serial Number: SL #2c
Date of Adoption: 15 Dec. 2003

Financial planning for any fiscal year or the remaining part of any fiscal year shall not deviate materially from elder board's ends priorities, risk fiscal jeopardy, or fail to be derived from a strategic plan.

Further, without limiting the scope of the foregoing by this enumeration, the senior pastor shall not allow budgeting that:

1. Risks incurring those situations or conditions described as unacceptable in the elder board policy "Financial Condition and Activities."
2. Omits conservative, credible projections of revenues, expenses, and cash flows based on historical and demographic data; omits separation of capital and operational items; or omits disclosure of planning assumptions.

3. Provides less for elder board prerogatives during the year than is set forth in the Cost of Governance policy.

Policy of the Board of Elders

Staff Limitations
Financial Conditions and Activities
Policy Serial Number: SL #2d
Date of Adoption: 15 Dec. 2003

With respect to the actual, ongoing financial condition and activities, the senior pastor shall not cause or allow the development of fiscal jeopardy or material deviation of actual expenditures from elder board priorities established in ends policies.

Further, without limiting the scope of the foregoing by this enumeration, the senior pastor shall not:

1. Expend more funds than have been received in the fiscal year to date unless the debt guideline (#2 below) is met (with the exception of building fund activities).
2. Incur short-term debt in an amount greater than can be repaid with unrestricted revenues within 120 days.
3. Allow the operating cash balance to fall below a target of the total necessary to fund thirty days' average operating expenditures (with the exception that the church shall not borrow additional, unnecessary funds to meet this requirement).
4. Incur any long-term debt or use any long-term restricted fund balances (i.e., funds designated for future capital projects).
5. Use any restricted fund balances for other than the designated purpose.
6. Expend any bequests in excess of $100,000 that are unrestricted by the donor.
7. Conduct inter-fund shifting in amounts greater than can be restored by unrestricted revenues within thirty days.
8. Fail to settle payroll and debts by the applicable legal due dates.
9. Allow tax payments or other government ordered payments or filings to be overdue or inaccurately filed.
10. Make a single purchase or enter into any contract of greater than 1 percent of planned annual operating expenditures. Splitting orders or payments to avoid this limit is not acceptable.
11. Acquire, encumber, or dispose of real property.

Policy of the Board of Elders

Staff Limitations
Asset Protection
Policy Serial Number: SL #2e
Date of Adoption: 15 Dec. 2003

The senior pastor shall not cause or allow church assets to be unprotected, inadequately maintained, or unnecessarily risked.

Further, without limiting the scope of the foregoing by this enumeration, the senior pastor shall not:

1. Fail to insure assets against theft and casualty losses to at least 90 percent replacement value.
2. Fail to insure against liability losses to elder board members and staff (director and officer insurance) and the organization itself in an amount greater than the average for comparable organizations.
3. Fail to carry adequate insurance to cover theft or dishonesty of employees and volunteers.
4. Subject plant and equipment to improper wear and tear or insufficient maintenance.
5. Unnecessarily expose the organization, its elder board, or staff to claims of liability.
6. Make any purchase: (a) wherein normally prudent protection has not been given against conflict of interest; (b) of over 1 percent of planned annual operating expenditures without having obtained comparative prices and quality; (c) of over 1 percent of planned annual operating expenditures without a stringent method of assuring the balance of long-term quality and cost. Orders or payments shall not be split to avoid these criteria.
7. Fail to protect information and files from loss or significant damage.
8. Receive, process, or disburse funds under controls that are insufficient to meet generally accepted standards.
9. Compromise the independence of the elder board's external monitoring or advice.
10. Invest or hold operating capital in insecure instruments, including deposits in uninsured or disreputable depository institutions and bonds of less than AA rating at any time, or in non-interest-bearing accounts except where necessary to facilitate ease in operational transactions.

11. Endanger the organization's public image, credibility, or its ability to accomplish ends.
12. Change the organization's name or substantially alter its identity in the community.
13. Create or purchase any subsidiary corporation.

Policy of the Board of Elders

Staff Limitations
Compensation and Benefits
Policy Serial Number: SL #2f
Date of Adoption: 15 Dec. 2003

With respect to employment, compensation, and benefits to employees, consultants, contract workers, and volunteers, the senior pastor shall not cause or allow jeopardy to fiscal integrity or to public image.

Further, without limiting the scope of the foregoing by this enumeration, he shall not:

1. Change the senior pastor's own compensation and benefits, except as his benefits are consistent with a package for all other employees.
2. Promise or imply permanent or guaranteed employment.
3. Establish current compensation and benefits that deviate materially from the geographic and/or peer group comparison from churches of like size for the skills employed.
4. Create obligations over a longer term than revenues can be safely projected, in no event longer than one year and in all events subject to losses in revenue.
5. Establish or change retirement benefits so as to cause unpredictable or inequitable situations, including those that:
    a. Provide less than some basic level of benefits to all full-time employees, though differential benefits to encourage longevity are not prohibited.
    b. Allow any employee to lose benefits already accrued from any foregoing plan.
    c. Treat the senior pastor differently from other key employees.

Policy of the Board of Elders

Staff Limitations
Ends Focus of Contracts
Policy Serial Number: SL #2g
Date of Adoption: 15 Dec. 2003

The senior pastor shall not enter into any contract arrangement that fails to emphasize the production of ends and the avoidance of unacceptable means.

Further, without limiting the scope of the foregoing by this enumeration, he shall not:

1. Enter into contracts or other business relationships of significant risk without review by more than one person qualified for such review.
2. Enter into a contract for paid endorsements of products or services.

Policy of the Board of Elders

Staff Limitations
Communication and Support to the Board
Policy Serial Number: SL #2h
Date of Adoption: 15 Dec. 2003

The senior pastor shall not permit the elder board to be uninformed or unsupported in its work.

Further, without limiting the scope of the foregoing by this enumeration, he shall not:

1. Neglect to submit required monitoring data (see policy "Monitoring Senior Pastor Performance") in a timely, accurate, understandable, nondefensive, and unbiased fashion, directly addressing provisions of elder board policies being monitored and justifying his interpretation.
2. Fail to report in a timely manner an actual or anticipated non-compliance with any policy of the elder board.
3. Neglect to submit decision information required periodically by the elder board or let the elder board be unaware of relevant trends.
4. Let the elder board be unaware of any incidental information it requires including anticipated media coverage, threatened or pending lawsuits, dismissals or requested resignations of paid staff, significant moral failures within the staff or at church related activities, and material internal changes.
5. Fail to advise the elder board if, in the senior pastor's opinion, the elder board is not in compliance with its own policies on governance process and board–senior pastor linkage, particularly in the case of elder board behavior that is detrimental to

the work relationship between the elder board and the senior pastor.

6. Present information in unnecessarily complex or lengthy form or in a form that fails to differentiate among information of three types: monitoring, decision preparation, and other incidental information.

7. Fail to provide a workable mechanism for official elder board, officer, or committee communications.

8. Fail to deal with the elder board as a whole except when (a) fulfilling individual requests for information or (b) responding to officers or committees duly charged by the elder board.

9. Fail to supply for the elder board's consent agenda decision items that have been delegated to the senior pastor but require elder board approval by law, regulation, or contract, such as housing allowances and appointment of a treasurer.

Policy of the Board of Elders

Staff Limitations
Doctrine and Practices
Policy Serial Number: SL #2i
Date of Adoption: 15 Dec. 2003

The senior pastor shall not allow conditions, procedures, or decisions that violate the clearly defined mandates of the Bible or LCBC's interpretation of the Bible as stipulated in the LCBC Constitution and Bylaws.

Further, without limiting the scope of the foregoing by enumeration, he shall not:

1. Knowingly permit the marriage of a divorced person to take place at the church or be officiated by a staff member unless the divorce was legitimate as defined in the Bible. That is, the divorce must have been legally granted and the ex-spouse of the divorced person seeking marriage must have been an unbeliever that abandoned a believing spouse or have committed adultery.

2. Encourage divorce under any circumstance or separation, except to protect innocent parties or as part of a process motivated by a desire for restoration in the marriage.

3. Permit nonbelievers, unbaptized persons, or those that have been ordained by churches whose doctrine is not compatible with LCBC's to perform baptisms at LCBC.

Policy of the Board of Elders

Staff Limitations
Style of Ministry
Policy Serial Number: SL #2j
Date of Adoption: 15 Dec. 2003

With respect to the entire operation of LCBC, the senior pastor shall not allow conditions, procedures, or decisions that interfere with or violate the chosen ministry style of LCBC.

Further, without limiting the scope of the foregoing by enumeration, he shall not:

1. Fail to produce an environment that encourages the unchurched to attend and begin a process of building a closer relationship with God.
2. Fail to foster an environment that promotes the spiritual growth of all believers.
3. Allow cultural barriers based on tradition or the personal tastes of those in the church to prevent the unchurched from being attracted to the church.
4. Allow inward focus to dominate outward vision.
5. Fail to use gentle and loving methods of correction.

Policy of the Board of Elders

Staff Limitations
Emergency Senior Pastor Succession
Policy Serial Number: SL #2k
Date of Adoption: 15 Dec. 2003

In order to protect LCBC and the elder board from the consequences of a sudden loss of the senior pastor, the senior pastor shall have no fewer than two other staff members sufficiently familiar with elder board and senior pastor issues and processes to enable either to take over with reasonable proficiency as an interim successor.

Policy of the Board of Elders

Governance Process
Global Governance Commitment
Policy Serial Number: GP #1
Date of Adoption: 15 Dec. 2003

The purpose of the elder board, on behalf of Lancaster County Bible Church partners and community in subjection to God, is to see to it that LCBC (a) achieves appropriate results for appropriate persons at an appropriate cost (as specified in elder board ends policies) and (b) avoids unacceptable actions and situations (as prohibited in elder board staff limitations policies).

Policy of the Board of Elders

Governance Process
Governing Style
Policy Serial Number: GP #2a
Date of Adoption: 15 Dec. 2003

The elder board will govern biblically with an emphasis on (a) outward vision rather than an internal preoccupation, (b) collective rather than individual decisions while permitting the expression of individual viewpoints, (c) strategic leadership more than administrative detail, (d) clear distinction of elder board and staff roles, (f) future rather than past or present, and (g) proactivity rather than reactivity.
Accordingly:

1. The elder board will cultivate a sense of group responsibility. The elder board, not the staff, will be responsible for excellence in governing. The elder board will be the initiator of board policy, not merely a reactor to staff initiatives. The elder board will not use the expertise of individual members to substitute for the judgment of the elder board, although the expertise of individual members may be used to enhance the understanding of the elder board as a body.
2. The elder board will direct, control, and inspire the organization through the careful establishment of broad written policies reflecting the elder board's interpretation of biblical mandates and the organization's values and perspectives. The elder board's major policy focus will be on the intended long-term impacts outside the staff organization, not on the administrative or programmatic means of attaining those effects.
3. The elder board will enforce upon itself whatever discipline is needed to govern with excellence. Discipline will apply to matters such as attendance, preparation for meetings, policy-making principles, respect of roles, and ensuring the continuance of governance capability. Although the elder board can change its governance

process policies at any time, it will observe those currently in force scrupulously.

4. Continual elder board development will include orientation of new elder board members in the elder board's governance process and periodic elder board discussion of process improvement.
5. The elder board will allow no officer, individual, or committee of the elder board to hinder or be an excuse for not fulfilling group obligations.
6. The elder board will monitor and discuss the elder board's process and performance at each meeting. Self-monitoring will include comparison of elder board activity and discipline to policies in the governance process and board-staff linkage categories.

Policy of the Board of Elders

Governance Process
Board Job Description
Policy Serial Number: GP #2b
Date of Adoption: 15 Dec. 2003

Specific job outputs of the elder board are those that fulfill the biblical requirements of overseeing and shepherding on behalf of the LCBC community (1 Peter 5:1–4).
Accordingly:

1. The elder board will establish an overarching vision for LCBC that is outwardly focused, strategic, and proactive.
2. The elder board will oversee LCBC in the achievement of appropriate organizational performance through the creation of:
   a. The structural, authoritative, and protective link between the LCBC partnership and community and the operational organization.
   b. Written governing policies that address the broadest levels of all organizational decisions and situations.
      i. Ends: Organizational impacts, benefits, outcomes, recipients, and their relative worth (what good for which recipients at what cost).
      ii. Staff Limitations: Constraints on staff authority that establish the prudence, ethics, and doctrinal boundaries within which all staff and organizational activity and decisions must take place.
      iii. Governance Process: Specification of how the elder board conceives, carries out, and monitors its own task.

   iv. Board-Staff Linkage: How power is delegated and its proper use monitored; the senior pastor role, authority, and accountability.

  c. Assurance of successful organizational performance on ends and staff limitations.

3. The elder board will shepherd by taking direct responsibility to:

  a. Maintain doctrinal purity among all ministry entities directly related to LCBC and encourage sound doctrine among all attendees (Titus 1:9).

  b. Be servant leaders, modeling Christlikeness to the LCBC community (1 Peter 5:3) and ensure that this is accomplished through mutual accountability within the board.

  c. Pray for the healing of the sick for those who directly request it of the elder board (James 5:14).

  d. Review and approve partnership applications from those who meet partnership qualifications.

  e. Provide for continuity of leadership by prayerfully selecting those who should be presented to the partnership for election to the elder board.

  f. Act on discipline and conflict resolution issues in which due process has been exhausted at the staff level. In acting on these issues, the elder board must:

   i. Approach discipline and conflict resolution matters in a spirit of gentleness and humility (Gal. 6:1–2) and without bias or partiality (1 Tim. 5:21).

   ii. Continue to ensure due process in discipline and conflict resolution matters as commanded in the New Testament (Matt. 18:15–20).

   iii. Assign at least one elder responsible for seeing the issue through to resolution. The assigned elder(s) represent(s) the elder board in meetings with parties involved in the issue, within the constraints determined by the board. The elder(s) responsible also act(s) as a communication conduit between the board and the individuals involved in the discipline or conflict resolution issue.

   iv. Make a final binding decision on discipline and conflict resolution issues that remain unresolved after due process has been exhausted at both the staff and board levels.

Governance Process
Agenda Planning
Policy Serial Number: GP #2c
Date of Adoption: 15 Dec. 2003

To accomplish its job products with a governance style consistent with elder board policies, the elder board will follow an annual agenda, which (a) completes a re-exploration of ends policies annually and (b) continually improves elder board performance through elder board education and enriched input and deliberation.

1. The cycle will conclude each year on the last day of September so that administrative planning and budgeting can be based on accomplishing a one-year segment of the elder board's most recent statement of long-term ends.
2. The cycle will start with the elder board's development of its agenda for the next year.
   a. Consultations with selected groups in the partnership and community, or other methods of gaining partnership and community input will be determined and arranged in the first quarter, to be held during the balance of the year.
   b. Governance education, and education related to ends determination (e.g., presentations by futurists, demographers, advocacy groups, staff, etc.) will be arranged in the first quarter, to be held during the balance of the year.
   c. Throughout the year, the elder board will attend to consent agenda items as expeditiously as possible.
   d. Senior pastor monitoring will be included on the agenda if monitoring reports show policy violations, or if policy criteria are to be debated.
   e. Senior pastor remuneration will be decided after a review of monitoring reports received in the last year during the month of October.

Governance Process
Board Chairman's Role
Policy Serial Number: GP #2d
Date of Adoption: 15 Dec. 2003

The board chairman, a specially empowered member of the elder board, assures the integrity of the elder board's process and, secondarily, occasionally represents the elder board to outside parties.

Accordingly:

1. The assigned result of the chairman's job is that the elder board behaves consistently with its own rules and those legitimately imposed upon it from outside the organization.

   a. Meeting discussion content will be on those issues that, according to elder board policy, clearly belong to the elder board to decide or to monitor.

   b. Information that is for neither monitoring performance nor elder board decisions will be avoided or minimized and always noted as such.

   c. Deliberation will be fair, open, and thorough, but also timely, orderly, and kept to the point.

2. The authority of the chairman consists in making decisions that fall within topics covered by elder board policies on governance process and board-staff linkage, with the exception of (a) employment or termination of a senior pastor and (b) where the elder board specifically delegates portions of this authority to others. The chairman is authorized to use any reasonable interpretation of the provisions in these policies.

   a. The chairman is empowered to chair elder board meetings with all the commonly accepted power of that position, such as ruling and recognizing.

   b. The chairman has no authority to make decisions about policies created by the elder board within ends and staff limitations policy areas. Therefore, the chairman has no authority to supervise or direct the senior pastor.

   c. The chairman may represent the elder board to outside parties in announcing elder board–stated positions and in stating chair decisions and interpretations within the area delegated to him.

   d. The chairman may delegate this authority but remains accountable for its use.

Policy of the Board of Elders

Governance Process
Board Members' Code of Conduct
Policy Serial Number: GP #2e
Date of Adoption: 15 Dec. 2003

The elder board commits itself and its members to biblically based, ethical, and lawful conduct.

1. Members must protect the interests of the partnership, unconflicted by loyalties to staff, other organizations, or their own personal interests.
2. Members must avoid conflict of interest with respect to their fiduciary responsibility.
   a. There will be no self-dealing or business by a member with the organization if the dealing or business is in excess of 5 percent of the individual's or organization's annual operating budget. Members will annually disclose their involvement with other organizations, with vendors, or any associations that might be or might reasonably be seen as being a conflict.
   b. When the elder board is to decide upon an issue, about which a member has an unavoidable conflict of interest, that member shall absent himself without comment from not only the vote, but also from the deliberation.
   c. Board members will not use their elder board position to obtain employment in the organization for themselves, family members, or close associates. Should an elder board member be presented to the board for possible employment or be offered employment, he must first resign from the elder board.
3. Board members may not attempt to exercise individual authority over the organization.
   a. Members' interaction with the senior pastor or with staff must recognize the lack of authority vested in individuals except when explicitly elder board authorized.
   b. Members' interaction with public, press, or other entities must recognize the same limitation and the inability of any elder board member to speak for the elder board except to repeat explicitly stated elder board decisions.
   c. Except for participation in elder board deliberation about whether the senior pastor has achieved any reasonable interpretation of elder board policy, members will not express individual judgments of performance of employees of the senior pastor.
4. Members will respect confidentiality appropriate to issues of a sensitive nature.
5. Members will be properly prepared for elder board deliberation.
6. Members will be involved in the church at a level consistent with the expectations for partnership.

7. Members will regularly attend board meetings. Unavoidable absences should be communicated to the chairman prior to the meeting.
8. A board member may be removed from the board by a majority vote of all the board members, for the following reasons.
   a. Moral failure
   b. Improper fiduciary disclosure
   c. Irregular meeting or worship attendance
   d. Failure to meet biblical qualifications
   e. Change in doctrinal views that deviate from LCBC's doctrine

Policy of the Board of Elders

Governance Process
Board Members' Qualifications
Policy Serial Number: GP #2f
Date of Adoption: 15 Dec. 2003

Specific elder board qualifications are those that are consistent with both biblical mandates found in 1 Timothy 3:1–13 and Titus 1:5–16 as well as leadership standards unique to the LCBC community.
Accordingly:

1. The following biblical mandates must be evident in individuals being considered for eldership.
   a. Claims a personal relationship with Christ
   b. Maintains an active relationship with Christ
   c. A good reputation with outsiders
   d. Able to teach
   e. Above reproach
   f. Controlled children
   g. Devout
   h. Free from the love of money
   i. Gentle, not contentious
   j. Hospitable
   k. Husband of one wife
   l. Just
   m. Lover of what is good
   n. Manager of his household
   o. Not a recent convert
   p. Not addicted to wine
   q. Not pugnacious
   r. Not quick-tempered

     s. Not self-seeking
     t. Prudent
     u. Respectable
     v. Sensitive
     w. Temperate
2. The following leadership qualities must be evident in individuals being considered for eldership.
     a. Proven record of leadership experience
     b. Able to think critically, abstractly, and globally through issues
     c. Able to receive and offer constructive criticism
     d. Possess the spiritual gifts of leadership and/or administration
3. The following qualifications unique to the LCBC community must be evident in individuals being considered for eldership.
     e. In agreement with the LCBC doctrinal statement
     f. In agreement with the LCBC constitution and bylaws
     g. In agreement with the LCBC philosophy and style of ministry
     h. In agreement with the elder board's chosen style of governance
     i. Able to identify and use personal spiritual gifts
     j. A proven track record of working well with people
     k. A desire to serve in various ministry capacities within LCBC
     l. Able to attend LCBC on a consistent basis
     m. A current LCBC partner
     n. General support from family members
     o. Willing to abstain from the use of tobacco and alcoholic beverages while on the elder board

Policy of the Board of Elders

Governance Process
Board Committee Principles
Policy Serial Number: GP #2g
Date of Adoption: 15 Dec. 2003

Board committees, when used, will be assigned so as to reinforce the wholeness of the elder board's job and so as never to interfere with delegation from elder board to senior pastor.
Accordingly:

1. Board committees are to help the elder board do its job, not to help or advise the staff. Committees ordinarily will assist the elder board by preparing policy alternatives and implications for elder board deliberation. In keeping with the elder board's broader focus,

elder board committees will normally not have direct dealings with current staff operations.

2. Board committees may not speak or act for the elder board except when formally given such authority for specific and time-limited purposes. Expectations and authority will be carefully stated in order not to conflict with authority delegated to the senior pastor.

3. Board committees cannot exercise authority over staff. Because the senior pastor works for the full elder board, he will not be required to obtain approval of an elder board committee before an executive action.

4. Board committees are to avoid overidentification with organizational parts rather than the whole. Therefore, an elder board committee that has helped the elder board create policy on some topic will not be used to monitor organizational performance on that same subject.

5. Committees will be used sparingly and ordinarily in an ad hoc capacity.

6. This policy applies to any group that is formed by elder board action, whether or not it is called a committee and regardless of whether the group includes elder board members. It does not apply to committees formed under the authority of the senior pastor.

Policy of the Board of Elders

Governance Process
Board Committee Structure
Policy Serial Number: GP #2h
Date of Adoption: 15 Dec. 2003

A committee is an elder board committee only if its existence and charge come from the elder board, regardless of whether elder board members sit on the committee. The only elder board committees are those that are set forth in this policy. Unless otherwise stated, a committee ceases to exist as soon as its task is complete.

Policy of the Board of Elders

Governance Process
Cost of Governance
Policy Serial Number: GP #2i
Date of Adoption: 15 Dec. 2003

Because poor governance costs more than learning to govern well, the elder board will invest in its governance capacity.

Accordingly:

1. Board skills, methods, and supports will be sufficient to assure governing with excellence.
   a. Training and retraining will be used liberally to maintain and increase existing members' skills and understanding.
   b. New member orientation will be intense and purposed in order to bring each member to a full understanding of the governance process. Orientation will begin for each new member when the member is approved by the partners and before the term begins. Candidates for membership will be given a general overview of the governance process.
   c. Outside monitoring assistance will be arranged so that the elder board can exercise confident control over organizational performance. This includes, but is not limited to, fiscal audit.
   d. Outreach mechanisms will be used as needed to ensure the elder board's ability to listen to partner and community viewpoints and values.
2. Costs will be prudently incurred, though not at the expense of endangering the development and maintenance of superior capability and communicated during the budget planning process.

Policy of the Board of Elders

Board-Staff Linkage
Global Board-Staff Linkage
Policy Serial Number: BSL #1
Date of Adoption: 15 Dec. 2003

The elder board's sole official connection to the operational organization, its achievements, and conduct will be through the senior pastor.

Policy of the Board of Elders

Board-Staff Linkage
Unity of Control
Policy Serial Number: BSL #2a
Date of Adoption: 15 Dec. 2003

Only officially passed motions of the elder board are binding on the senior pastor.

Accordingly:

1. Decisions or instructions of individual elder board members, officers, or committees are not binding on the senior pastor except in rare instances when the elder board has specifically authorized such exercise of authority.
2. In the case of elder board members or committees requesting information or assistance without elder board authorization, the senior pastor can refuse such requests that require, in the senior pastor's opinion, a material amount of staff time or funds or is disruptive.

Policy of the Board of Elders

Board-Staff Linkage
Accountability of the Senior Pastor
Policy Serial Number: BSL #2b
Date of Adoption: 15 Dec. 2003

The senior pastor is the elder board's only link to operational achievement and conduct, so that all authority and accountability of paid and volunteer staff, as far as the elder board is concerned, is considered the authority and accountability of the senior pastor.

Accordingly:

1. The elder board will never give instructions related to job responsibility to persons who report directly or indirectly to the senior pastor.
2. The elder board will not formally evaluate the job performance of any paid or volunteer staff other than the senior pastor. The elder board's evaluation of staff members for licensing or ordination will not be considered to be an evaluation of job performance.
3. Organizational accomplishment of elder board stated ends and avoidance of elder board proscribed means will be viewed as successful senior pastor performance.

Policy of the Board of Elders

Board-Staff Linkage
Delegation to the Senior Pastor
Policy Serial Number: BSL #2c
Date of Adoption: 15 Dec. 2003

The elder board will instruct the senior pastor through written policies that prescribe the organizational ends to be achieved and describe organizational situations and actions to be avoided, allowing the senior pastor to use any reasonable interpretation of these policies.

Accordingly:

1. The elder board will develop policies instructing the senior pastor to achieve specified results, for specified recipients at a specified cost. These policies will be developed systematically from the broadest, most general level to more defined levels, and will be called ends policies. All issues that are not ends issues as defined above are means issues.

2. The elder board will develop policies that limit the latitude the senior pastor may exercise in choosing the organizational means. These policies will be developed systematically from the broadest, most general level to more defined levels, and they will be called staff limitations policies. The elder board will never prescribe organizational means.

3. As long as the senior pastor uses *any reasonable interpretation* of the elder board's ends and staff limitations policies, the senior pastor is authorized to establish all further policies, make all decisions, take all actions, establish all practices, and develop all activities. Such decisions of the senior pastor shall have full force and authority as if decided by the elder board.

4. The elder board may change its ends and staff limitations policies, thereby shifting the boundary between elder board and senior pastor domains. By doing so, the elder board changes the latitude of choice given to the senior pastor. But as long as any particular delegation is in place, the elder board will respect and support the senior pastor's choices.

Policy of the Board of Elders

Board-Staff Linkage
Monitoring Senior Pastor Performance
Policy Serial Number: BSL #2d
Date of Adoption: 15 Dec. 2003

Systematic and rigorous monitoring of the senior pastor's job performance will be solely against the only expected senior pastor job outputs: organizational accomplishment of elder board policies on ends and organizational operation within the boundaries established in elder board policies on staff limitations.

Accordingly:

1. Monitoring is simply to determine the degree to which elder board policies are being met. Information that does not do this will not be considered to be monitoring information.
2. The elder board will acquire monitoring data by one or more of three methods: (a) by internal report, in which the senior pastor discloses compliance information, along with his/her justification for the reasonableness of interpretation; (b) by external report, in which an external, disinterested third party selected by the elder board assesses compliance with policies, augmented with the senior pastor's justification for the reasonableness of his/her interpretation; and (c) by direct elder board inspection, in which a designated member or members of the elder board assess compliance with policy, with access to the senior pastor's justification for the reasonableness of his/her interpretation.
3. In every case, the standard for compliance shall be *any reasonable senior pastor interpretation* of the elder board policy being monitored. The elder board is final arbiter of reasonableness but will always judge with a "reasonable person" test rather than with interpretations favored by elder board members or by the elder board as a whole.
4. All policies that instruct the senior pastor will be monitored at a frequency and by a method chosen by the elder board. The elder board can monitor any policy at any time by any method but will ordinarily depend on the following routine schedule.

Policy	Method	Frequency
Ministry Style	TBD	TBD
Treatment of Attendees	TBD	TBD
Treatment of Staff	TBD	TBD
Financial Planning/Budgeting	TBD	TBD
Financial Condition and Activities	TBD	TBD
Emergency Senior Pastor Succession	TBD	TBD
Compensation and Benefits	TBD	TBD
Communication and Support	TBD	TBD
Direct Inspection	TBD	TBD

Policy of the Board of Elders

Ends
Temporary
Policy Serial Number: E #1
Date of Adoption: 15 Dec. 2003

Pending further elder board determinations, *ends* of the organization will remain as previously stated explicitly by the elder board or as found implicitly in previously adopted elder board documents.

Used by permission

ELDER BOARD
POLICY MANUAL

*T*his is the policy manual for a large church located in the United States that wished to remain anonymous but was willing for its manual to appear in this book.

Chapter 1 Governance Policy

Global Policy

The purpose of the elder board is to be accountable to God to shepherd [this] church while avoiding unscriptural actions or situations or violating the bylaws.

Governance Style

The elders will govern with an emphasis on (1) demonstrating Christlike character, (2) outward vision rather than internal preoccupation, (3) encouragement of diversity of gifts, (4) strategic leadership more than administrative detail, (5) clear distinction of elder board and senior pastor roles, (6) collective rather than individual decisions, (7) future rather than past or present, and (8) proactivity rather than reactivity.

Accordingly:

1. The elder board will cultivate a sense of group responsibility. The elder board, not the staff, will be responsible for excellence in governing. The elder board will be the initiator of policy, not merely a reactor to staff initiatives. The elder board will use the expertise of individual elders to enhance the ability of the elder board as a body rather than to substitute individual judgments for the elder board's values. The elder board will allow no officer, individual, or committee of the elder board to hinder or be an excuse for not fulfilling elder board commitments.

2. The elder board will direct, oversee, and inspire the congregation through the careful establishment of broad written policies reflecting the elder board's values and perspectives about ends to be achieved and means to be avoided. The elder board's major policy focus will be on intended long-term effects not on the administrative or programmatic means of attaining those effects.

3. The elder board will enforce upon itself whatever discipline is needed to govern with excellence. Discipline will apply to matters such as attendance, preparation, policy-making principles, respect for roles, and ensuring continuance of governance capability. Continual elder board development will include orientation of new elders in the elder board's governance process and periodic elder board discussion of process improvement.

4. The elder board will monitor and discuss the elder board's process and performance at each meeting. Self-monitoring will include comparison of elder board activity and discipline to the policies in the governance process, the elder board–senior pastor linkage, and ends policy categories.

5. The elders are committed to unity. In keeping with this commitment, all questions or issues under consideration not requiring a formal motion and vote as set forth in the section entitled "Role of the Elder Board Secretary" are discussed until everyone comes to a consensus agreement. If, however, the board is unable to reach consensus, the question will be tabled until the next formal board meeting, when the matter will again be considered. At that time, after thorough discussion and prayer, if no more than 20 percent are opposed to the question, it shall be considered adopted. All elders are then committed to supporting the question.

Elder Board Job Description

The specific job of the elder board is to define "ends," explicitly write policies, and appropriately monitor those policies.

Accordingly:

1. The elder board will produce the link between itself and the congregation.
2. The elder board will produce written governing policies that, at the broadest levels, address each category of organizational decision.
   a. Ends: organizational products, effects, outcomes, recipients, and their relative worth, i.e., what benefit, for whom, and at what cost.
   b. Executive Limitations: constraints on executive authority that establish the prudence and ethics boundaries within which all executive activity and decisions must take place.
   c. Governance Process: specification of how the elder board conceives, carries out, and monitors its own task.
   d. Elder Board–Senior Pastor Linkage: how power is delegated and its proper use monitored; authority and accountability of the senior pastor role.
3. The elder board will produce assurance of senior pastor performance (against policies described in 2a and 2b above).
4. The elder board will reexplore ends policies annually, at a minimum.
5. The elder board will continually strive to improve its performance through education, enriching input, team-building experiences, and deliberation.
6. The cycle will begin each January as the new elder board takes office and conclude each year on the last day of December.
   a. Consultations with selected groups in the congregation or other methods of gaining congregational input will generally be determined and arranged in the first quarter, to be held during the balance of the year.
   b. Governance education and training related to ends determination (for example, presentations by futurists, demographers, advocacy groups, other staff, etc.) will be arranged for as needs and opportunities are identified and approved by the board.
7. Throughout the year, the elder board will attend to agenda items as expeditiously as possible.

Selection of Board Officers

The elder board requires a chairman and other officers to set specific goals and agenda items, assure policies and processes are being honored, and occasionally act as representative to other parties. The elder board will elect new officers each year.

Accordingly:

1. The selection process for chairman will take place not later than the October elder board meeting. Each nominee will indicate to the elder board if he feels called to accept this charge and may indicate why he believes he would make a strong chairman.
2. The elder board will then make its selection by secret ballot. The winner must receive all except 20 percent or two votes, whichever is the greater number of opposing votes.
3. No later than the November meeting, the on-coming chairman will make a recommendation to the elder board for vice chairman and secretary. The elder board will approve those selections and the successful nominee must receive all except 20 percent or two votes, whichever is the greater number of opposing votes.
4. During the December meeting, the new chairman will present an agenda for discussion and decision making for the coming year.

Role of the Board Chairman

The chairman assures the integrity and fulfillment of the elder board's process, and secondarily, occasionally represents the elder board to outside parties.

Accordingly:

1. The job result of the chairman is that the elder board behaves consistently with its own rules and those legitimately imposed upon it from outside the organization.
   a. Meeting discussion content will consist of those issues that, according to Elder Board Governance Policy, clearly belong to the elder board to determine, not the senior pastor. The senior pastor or any elder may request an item be included on the agenda of the next meeting at any time. The agenda will be prepared and distributed by the elder board chairman.
   b. The chairman will assure deliberation is fair, open, and thorough and also timely, orderly, and to the point.
2. The authority of the chairman consists in making decisions that fall within topics covered by elder board policies on governance

process and board–senior pastor linkage, except where the elder board specifically delegates portions of this authority to others. The chairman is authorized to use any reasonable interpretation of the provisions in these policies.

3. The chairman is empowered to chair elder board meetings with all the commonly accepted power of that position (for example: ruling, recognizing).

4. The chairman has no authority to make decisions about policies created by the elder board within the ends and executive limitations policy areas.

5. The chairman has no authority to supervise or direct the senior pastor; however, the two should meet at least monthly to ensure continuity of activities and to advise each other of situations that are in progress or upcoming.

6. The chairman may represent the elder board to outside parties in announcing elder board–stated positions and in stating chair decisions and interpretations within the area delegated to him.

7. The chairman may delegate his authority but remains accountable for its use.

Elder Code of Conduct

The elders commit themselves individually and as a group collectively to Christlike conduct.

Accordingly:

1. An elder must represent loyalty, which does not conflict with interests of the congregation. This accountability supersedes any conflicting loyalty such as that to advocacy or interest groups and membership on other boards or staffs. It also supersedes the personal interest of any elder acting as a member of the congregation.

2. An elder must avoid conflict of interest with respect to his fiduciary responsibility.

   a. There must be no self-dealing or any conduct of private business or personal services between any elder and the church except as procedurally controlled, to assure openness, competitive opportunity, and equal access to inside information.

   b. When the elder board is to decide upon an issue about which he has an unavoidable conflict of interest, that elder shall excuse himself without comment from voting or deliberation.

   c. An elder must not use his position to obtain employment for himself, family members, or close associates. Should an elder pursue employment with the church, he must first resign his term.
   d. An elder will annually disclose his involvement with other organizations, vendors, or any other associations that might produce a conflict.
3. An elder may not attempt to exercise individual authority over the congregation or staff except as explicitly set forth in elder board policies.
   a. An elder must recognize the same limitations and the inability of any elder to speak for the elder board except to repeat explicitly stated elder board decisions.
   b. An elder will respect the confidentiality appropriate to issues of a sensitive nature.

Elder Board Committee Principles

Elder board committees, when used, shall serve the needs and purposes of the elder board and not interfere with delegation from the elder board to the senior pastor.
Accordingly:

1. Elder board committees are to help the elder board do its job, never to help or to advise the staff. Committees ordinarily will assist the elder board by preparing policy alternatives and implications for elder board deliberation. In keeping with the elder board's broader focus, elder board committees will normally not have dealings with current staff operations.
2. Elder board committees may not speak or act for the elder board except when formally given such authority for specific and time-limited purposes. Expectations and authority will be carefully stated in order not to conflict with authority delegated to the senior pastor.
3. Elder board committees cannot exercise authority over staff. Because the senior pastor works for the full elder board, he will not be required to obtain approval of an elder board committee before an executive action.
4. Elder board committees are to avoid overidentification with congregational parts rather than the whole. Therefore an elder board committee that has helped the elder board create a policy on some topic will not be used to monitor congregational performance on the same topic.

5. Committees will be used sparingly and ordinarily in an ad hoc capacity.
6. This policy applies to any group that is formed by elder board action, whether or not it is called a committee and regardless of whether the group includes elders. It does not apply to committees formed under the authority of the senior pastor.

Cost of Governance

Because poor governance costs more than learning to govern well, the elder board will invest in its governance ability and capacity. Accordingly:

1. Elder board skills, methods, and supports will be sufficient to assure governing with excellence.
   a. Training and retraining will be used liberally to orient new elders and candidates for eldership, as well as to maintain and increase existing elder skills and understandings.
   b. Outside monitoring assistance may be arranged so that the elder board can exercise confident control over staff performance.
   c. Outreach mechanisms may be used as needed to ensure the elder board's ability to listen to congregational viewpoints and values.
2. Costs will be prudently incurred, though not at the expense of endangering the development and maintenance of superior capability.

Role of the Elder Board Secretary

In general, the secretary is responsible for recording and disseminating minutes of all decision-making meetings (specifically board meetings and congregational meetings). He is also occasionally required to sign legal documents.
Accordingly:

1. With respect to certain legal matters, documented decisions must include a formal motion, a second, and a record of the vote. The matters that require such formal documentation may include:
   a. Approval of church polices.
   b. Approval of buying or selling property.
   c. Approval for borrowing money, including amount and loan terms.

    d. Approval of staff housing allowances. (These must be approved and recorded in the minutes before the fact, e.g., request for housing allowance recorded in the minutes of the June meeting would take effect July 1.)

    e. Approval of salary adjustments. (Because individual salaries are confidential, they can be reviewed at an elder board meeting without lists of individual salaries leaving the meeting. However, a record of the approved salaries must be attached as a confidential addendum to the minutes on file in the church office.)

    f. Approval of monetary expenditures in excess of the amount specified in Executive Limitations/Financial Conditions and Activities, section 5.

2. Elder board minutes are confidential and access to them is limited to the elders and selected members of senior staff. However, sometimes decisions on financial matters are made, which the finance department needs in writing. In situations such as this, the secretary should forward information pertinent to those specific details that the finance department legally requires, not the complete set of minutes. The senior pastor and chairman of the elders should also receive copies of this addendum.

3. The church bylaws require an elder be removed from the elder board if he is absent from three consecutive, regularly scheduled business meetings. (Anytime an elder is providentially absent from a meeting, that meeting shall not be counted as a missed meeting for the purpose of removal from office.) For this reason, the names of everyone in attendance, as well as absentees, should be listed in the minutes.

4. [The church's] elder board uses the minutes as a leadership tool. To this end, the secretary will record topics with sufficient detail so that a person who did not attend could read them and have a general understanding of what transpired.

5. After approval of the minutes, the secretary shall deliver the signed original copy of the minutes, along with appropriate attachments, to the senior pastor's executive assistant, who shall ensure the minutes are retained.

Elder Board Business Meetings

The elder board shall officially meet twice per month. One meeting shall be convened principally for a time of prayer. The second meeting shall be held to conduct normal board and church business. Three elders shall convene other meetings, which shall be considered special meetings, at the call of the chairman, or if they desire a meeting, but the chairman chooses not to call the meeting.

Chapter 2 Executive Limitations

Global Policy

The senior pastor shall not cause or allow any practice, activity, decision, or organizational circumstance that is either unlawful, imprudent, unethical, unscriptural, or contrary to the board-stated ends policy.

Treatment of Church Members

With respect to interactions with church members or those considering or applying to be church members, the senior pastor shall not cause or allow conditions, procedures, or decisions that are unsafe, undignified, unnecessarily intrusive or that fail to provide appropriate confidentiality or privacy.

Accordingly, the senior pastor shall not:

1. Use application forms that elicit information for which there is no clear necessity.
2. Use methods of collecting, reviewing, transmitting, or storing member information that fail to protect against improper access to the material elicited.

Treatment of Staff

With respect to the treatment of paid or volunteer staff, or those considering or applying to be paid or volunteer staff, the senior pastor shall not cause or allow conditions, procedures, or decisions that are unsafe, unfair, or undignified or that fail to provide appropriate confidentiality or privacy.

Accordingly, the senior pastor shall not:

1. Operate without written personnel policies that clarify personnel rules for staff. These policies shall include, but not be limited to:
   a. Procedures and processes to be followed when hiring new staff members.
   b. A method of monitoring performance of each staff member, which ties compensation to performance.
   c. A method of handling staff grievances of all natures.

d. A method of handling disciplinary actions, which include a full range of disciplinary actions from verbal counseling to termination. The senior pastor shall notify the elder board at its next regularly scheduled meeting of any disciplinary action pending or taken against any employee who is ordained or licensed. Further, the elder board shall be notified at its next regularly scheduled meeting of any disciplinary action taken against any employee, the next level of which is termination. The senior pastor may cause the termination of any employee at any time, if in his opinion good order or discipline is endangered. The elder board chairman shall immediately be notified if this action is taken.

e. Establish a standard of behavior for all employees. For ordained or licensed employees, these standards shall be similar to biblical principles established for elders. In addition, the procedure shall preclude staff from accepting gifts from congregational members other than those that are considered of minor value.

f. A requirement to prevent or protect against wrongful conditions of nepotism.

2. Discriminate against any staff member for expressing an ethical dissent.

3. Prevent staff from grieving to the board when: (1) internal grievance procedures have been exhausted, or (2) the employee alleges either that (a) board policy has been violated to his or her detriment or (b) board policy does not adequately protect his or her human rights.

4. Fail to acquaint staff with their rights under this policy.

5. Have two or more members of the same family, irrespective of the job classifications of any of the positions, employed by the church without the prior approval of the elder board.

Financial Plans and Budgeting

Financial planning for any fiscal year or the remaining part of any fiscal year shall not deviate materially from the board's ends priorities, risk fiscal jeopardy, or fail to be derived from current multiyear planning.

Accordingly, the senior pastor shall not allow budgeting that:

1. Contains too little information to enable credible projection of revenues and expenses, separation of capital and operational items, cash flow and disclosure of planning assumptions.

2. Plans the expenditure in any fiscal year of more funds than are projected in faith to be received in that period, unless the funds have been designated for expenditure in that period.
3. Reduces the current nonrestricted assets at any time to less than two weeks of then-projected weekly revenues.
4. Provides less for board prerogatives during the year than is set forth in the Cost of Governance policy.

Financial Conditions and Activities

With respect to the actual, ongoing financial conditions and activities, the senior pastor shall not cause or allow deviation from generally accepted accounting principles, or the development of fiscal jeopardy or a material or substantial deviation of actual expenditures from board priorities established in the ends policies.

Accordingly, the senior pastor shall not:

1. Expend more funds than are available in the fiscal year to date.
2. Fail to settle payroll and debts in a timely manner.
3. Move dedicated funds between accounts that would materially degrade ends policies, without board approval.
4. Allow tax payments or other government-ordered payments or filings to be overdue or inaccurately filed.
5. Authorize a single capital purchase of greater than $20,000 or make a commitment of any kind of greater than $7,500 other than budgeted personnel actions.
6. Purchase, encumber, or dispose of real property.

Emergency Senior Pastor Succession

In order to protect the church from sudden loss of senior pastor services, the senior pastor shall prepare no fewer than two other staff members familiar with elder board and senior pastor issues and processes.

Asset Protection

The senior pastor shall not allow the assets of the church to be unprotected, inadequately maintained, or unnecessarily risked.

Accordingly, the senior pastor shall not:

1. Fail to insure against theft and casualty losses to at least 80 percent of replacement value and against liability losses to elders, staff, and the church. This shall include the preparation, publication,

and distribution to staff of policies regarding the proper use and safeguarding of church funds and assets.

2. Subject building, fixtures, and equipment to improper wear and tear or insufficient maintenance.
3. Make any expenditure wherein reasonably prudent protection has not been given against conflict of interest.
4. Make any expenditure without a stringent method of assuring the balance of long-term quality and cost.
5. Fail to appropriately protect intellectual property, information and files (physical/electronic), from loss of significant damage.
6. Receive, process, or disburse funds under controls that are insufficient to meet the board-appointed auditor's standards.
7. Invest or hold operating capital church funds in insecure instruments. Day-to-day operating funds may be held in noninterest-bearing accounts; however, funds not needed for immediate use (two months) shall be invested in interest-bearing accounts.
8. Endanger the church's public image or credibility, particularly in ways that would hinder its accomplishment of ends policies.

Compensation and Benefits

With respect to employment, compensation, and benefits to employees, consultants, contract workers, and volunteers, the senior pastor shall not cause or allow jeopardy to fiscal integrity or public image.

Accordingly, the senior pastor shall not:

1. Change his own compensation and benefits.
2. Promise or imply permanent employment; that is, all employees shall be considered at-will employees.
3. Establish employee compensation ranges and benefits that deviate materially from the geographic or comparable market for the skills employed, without elder board approval.
4. Create compensation obligations over a longer term than revenues can be safely projected, in no event longer than one year, and in all events subject to losses in revenue.
5. Establish or change benefits.

Communication and Support to the Elder Board

The senior pastor shall not permit the elders to be uninformed or unsupported in their work.

Accordingly, the senior pastor shall not:

1. Neglect to submit monitoring data required by the elder board (see policy on Monitoring Senior Pastor Performance) in a timely, accurate, and understandable fashion, directly addressing provisions of elder board policies being monitored.
2. Let the elder board be unaware of events, which may have a significant and adverse impact upon the church's public image or credibility.
3. Fail to advise the elder board if, in the senior pastor's opinion, the elder board is not in compliance with its own policies on governance process and elder board–senior pastor linkage, particularly in the case of elder board behavior that is detrimental to the work relationship between the elder board and the senior pastor.
4. Fail to provide to the elder board as many staff and external points of view and options as needed regarding issues being considered by the elder board.
5. Fail to provide a mechanism for official elder board, officer, or committee communications.
6. Fail to deal with the elder board as a whole except when (a) fulfilling individual requests for information or (b) responding to officers or committees duly charged by the elder board.
7. Fail to report in a timely manner an actual or anticipated non-compliance with any policy of the elder board.
8. Fail to supply for the consent agenda all items delegated to the senior pastor yet required by law or contract to be elder board–approved, along with the monitoring assurance pertaining thereto.

Biblical Integrity

The senior pastor shall not cause or allow any teaching, practice, or conduct that is contrary to commonly accepted historic orthodox Christianity.

Chapter 3 Board-Staff Linkage

Global Policy

The elder board's sole official connection to the paid or volunteer staff, its achievement and conduct, shall be through the senior pastor.

Unity of Control

Only those decisions of the elder board as a body shall be binding on the senior pastor.
Accordingly:

1. Decisions or instructions of individual elders or committees
   are not binding on the senior pastor except in rare instances
   when the elder board has specifically authorized such exercise
   of authority.
   a. In the case of elders or committees requesting information
      or assistance without elder board authorization, the senior
      pastor can refuse such requests that require, in the senior
      pastor's opinion, a material amount of staff time or funds, or
      are disruptive.

Senior Pastor Accountability

Only the senior pastor shall be accountable to the elder board regarding staff achievement and conduct.
Accordingly:

1. The elder board will never give instructions to persons who report
   directly or indirectly to the senior pastor.
2. The elder board will refrain from evaluating, either formally or
   informally, any staff other than the senior pastor.
3. The elder board will view senior pastor performance as identical to staff performance, so that staff accomplishment of elder
   board–stated ends within the confines of executive limitations.

Delegation to the Senior Pastor

The elder board shall instruct the senior pastor through written policies that prescribe the ends to be achieved and describe the situations and actions to be avoided, allowing the senior pastor to use any reasonable interpretations of these polices.
Accordingly:

1. The elder board will develop and monitor polices instructing the
   senior pastor to achieve certain results, for certain recipients, at
   a specified cost. These policies will be developed systematically
   from the broadest, most general level to more defined levels, and
   will be called "Ends Policies."
2. The elder board will develop and monitor policies that limit the
   latitude the senior pastor may exercise in achieving ends policies.
   These policies will be developed systematically from the broadest most general level to more defined levels, and will be called
   "Executive Limitations Policies."
3. So long as the senior pastor uses any reasonable interpretation
   of the Ends Policies and Executive Limitations Policies, he is

authorized to establish any further policies, make all decisions, take all actions, establish all practices, and develop all activities in order to fulfill his responsibilities as described in paragraphs 1 and 2 above.

4. The elder board may change its Ends Policies and Executive Limitations Policies, thereby shifting the boundary between elder board and senior pastor domains. By doing so, the elder board changes the latitude of choice given to the senior pastor. However, as long as any particular delegation is in place, the elder board will respect and support the senior pastor's choices.

Monitoring Performance of the Senior Pastor

Systematic and rigorous monitoring of the senior pastor's job performance shall be solely against the accomplishment of elder board policies on ends and operation within the boundaries established in elder board policies on executive limitations.

Accordingly:

1. Monitoring is simply to determine the degree to which elder board policies are being met. Data that does not do this will not be considered to be monitoring data.
2. The elder board will acquire monitoring data by one or more of the following three methods or other appropriate methods:
   a. By internal report, in which the senior pastor discloses compliance information to the elder board.
   b. By external report, in which an external, disinterested third party selected by the elder board assesses compliance with elder board policies.
   c. By direct elder board inspection, in which an elder board–designated elder or elders assess compliance with the appropriate policy criteria.
3. In every case, the standard for compliance shall be any reasonable senior pastor interpretation of the elder board policy being monitored. Such interpretation shall be provided to the elder board from time to time, and the senior pastor shall advise the elder board whenever his interpretation changes or is modified.
4. All Ends Policies and Executive Limitations Polices will be monitored at a frequency and by a method chosen by the elder board. The elder board can monitor any policy at any time by any method, but will ordinarily depend on a routine schedule.

5. Senior pastor monitoring through review and approval of the Senior Pastor Monitoring Report will normally be included on each regularly scheduled elder board meeting agenda.
6. Senior pastor remuneration will be decided in April after a review of monitoring reports received since the last review was conducted. Any compensation changes shall be effective on the July 1 following completion of the review.

Chapter 4 Ends

Global Policy

[This church] exists to partner with God to produce an ever-increasing number of fully devoted followers of Jesus Christ.

Strategic Purpose

God's design for his church is for each Christ-follower to experience a process of continual growth and transformation into the likeness of Jesus (Rom. 8:29; 12:2) in the context of biblical community (Acts 2:42–47; 20:20; Rom. 12:10; Heb. 10:25). [This church] strives toward this goal through a fivefold strategic purpose:

Evangelism	communicating God's Son
Exaltation	celebrating God's presence
Edification	constructing God's people
Extension	channeling God's resources
Encouragement	caring for God's family

Evangelism

Evangelism is communicating the good news of God's Son, Jesus Christ, for the reconciliation of all people to God (Matt. 28:19; John 3:16; Rom. 6:23; 2 Cor. 5:18; Titus 3:5).

Accordingly, [this church] will:

1. Regularly provide members and attendees clear instruction on how to obtain forgiveness for sin and be reconciled to God through a personal relationship with Jesus Christ. We value using culturally relevant methods that cause people to recognize their need for God, and motivate them to be drawn into the body of Christ. We recognize that the Holy Spirit is the agent of change and that our responsibility is to intentionally convey the message of Christ

and create an environment in which the Holy Spirit can work to transform human hearts.

2. Seek to appeal primarily to the unchurched population of [our community]. However, since we recognize that Christ's commission is to disciple to the ends of the earth, [this church] will also maintain an appropriate focus on regional and global missions.

3. Offer to all who have accepted Christ, sufficient nurturing, spiritual training, and shepherding to cause them to make a public statement of faith by being obedient to Christ through baptism by immersion.

4. Equip believers to share their faith, and encourage them to seek opportunities to do so.

Exaltation

Exaltation is glorifying God the Father, God the Son, and God the Holy Spirit, and enjoying his presence with all of one's heart, soul, mind, and strength (John 4:24; Matt. 22:37–38; Ps. 9:1; Eccles. 12:13; Ps. 37:4; Ps. 150).

Accordingly, [this church] will:

1. Stress the core belief that God is spirit and those who worship him must worship in spirit and truth.

2. Plan and offer regular opportunities for experiencing the presence of God in corporate worship.

3. Encourage the practice of personal worship and provide practical biblical teaching on its importance and transforming impact.

Edification

Edification is discipling God's people to grow to full devotion to Christ through appropriate biblical teaching, authentic community, and the practice of personal spiritual disciplines (Col. 1:27; 1 Peter 2:2–3; Heb. 6:1–3; Phil. 1:9–10; Rom. 14:19; Eph. 5:1–2; Rom. 12:10; Gal. 6:3; Matt. 28:20).

Accordingly, [this church] will:

1. Provide appropriate biblical teaching for all ages and for all levels of spiritual maturity,
   a. Using a variety of settings, such as formal classroom, informal home small groups, one-on-one discipling/ mentoring relationships, and others.

   b. Using a variety of delivery methods, such as lecture, discussion, audio, video, computer-based learning, and others.
   c. Using studies and materials, which are developmentally appropriate according to age and spiritual maturity.
2. Provide opportunities for authentic community for all people,
   a. Using small groups as the prime means of connecting people together where they will receive care and shepherding and develop meaningful Christian relationships.
   b. Using task groups/ministry teams. As often as possible, ministry will happen in teams so that community can be developed in the context of working together.
   c. Using larger group "mezzanine" events such as conferences, retreats, classes, regular gatherings of particular life-stage groups, mission trips, etc., not only as entry-level opportunities to explore community at [this church] but as a means of enriching and enhancing relationships and lives.
   d. Using appropriate groups and teams to strengthen and improve marriage relationships, parenting skills, and other aspects of Christian life.
3. Provide appropriate teaching and tools to equip believers to grow in the spiritual disciplines such as prayer, worship, Bible study, journaling, giving, service, fasting, etc.

Extension

Extension is actively demonstrating God's love through the use of our unique individual passions, spiritual gifts, personal style, and resources to meet the needs of the body of Christ and the world (Matt. 22:37–38; Rom. 12:4–8; 1 Cor. 12:4–6; Gal. 5:6, 13; Eph. 4:11–12; Phil. 2:4; 1 Peter 4:10).
Accordingly, [this church] will:

1. Operate under the New Testament model of a "priesthood of all believers" (1 Peter 2:9–10), in which every Christ-follower discovers, develops, and uses his/her God-given spiritual gifts in ministry to others.
2. Identify Christ-followers with equipping gifts and place them in roles that enable them to prepare and train those with serving gifts (Eph. 4:11–12). Likewise, those with serving gifts must be placed in roles that enable them to serve.
3. Provide biblical teaching designed to assist each Christ-follower in discovering his/her unique blend of spiritual giftedness, passions,

and personal style. Provide opportunities for each Christ-follower
to utilize his/her gifts in ministry.
4. Encourage individuals to engage in only one or two areas of service commitment (rather than serving in many areas), in order to
   minister with excellence and maintain balance.
5. Ensure a congregational understanding that all of our resources—
   money, time, and talents—belong to God, and use of these resources
   should be guided by kingdom priorities.

Encouragement

Encouragement encompasses acts, which inspire hope, instill confidence, lift spirits, and provide needed support in a way that fosters a
sense of genuine care and belonging. Such acts exemplify God's own
love for humanity modeled by Jesus himself and commanded for the
New Testament church to follow, in order to care for God's family (Mark
9:41; Rom. 12:10, 13, 15; Gal. 6:2; 1 Thess. 5:14b; Heb. 3:13; 10:24; James
2:15–17; 1 Peter 4:8).

Accordingly, [this church] will:

1. Emphasize that the primary level of pastoral care can and should take
   place within the context of a biblical small-group community.
2. Provide training, support, and opportunities for service to individuals within the [church] family, especially those who are
   gifted in the areas of encouragement, mercy, intercession, and
   the like.
3. Provide biblical teaching designed to communicate the value and
   importance of caring for one another and encouraging one another
   in the name of Jesus Christ.
4. Oversee and provide assistance to the maintenance of self-supporting
   and self-sustaining ministries led primarily by volunteers. Examples
   might include:
   a. Various support and recovery groups.
   b. Intercessor prayer ministries.
   c. Recurring marriage enrichment courses.
   d. Ministries to prisoners, homeless, troubled youth, etc.
5. Organize and operate ministries that offer appropriate care
   and encouragement of an institutional nature. Examples might
   include:
   a. Pastoral counseling and professional referrals.
   b. Crisis care and pastor-on-call services.
   c. Neighborhood food pantry.
   d. Other specialized needs of the church and local community.

Appendix

The documents that follow have been approved by the elder board of [this church] and are intended to be consistent with the governance policies of the church.

In order to reduce confusion, these documents will be referred to as Working Polices or Working Policy Forms. They differ from governance polices in the following ways:

- They may be for reference only.
- They are often event—or problem—specific.
- They are more likely to be subject to change or elimination.
- These policies are defined as policies of [this church], hence the senior pastor will apply and enforce them just as though they were contained in the Governance Policy Manual of the church.

Shepherding Responsibilities

Each elder will be prepared to faithfully and diligently perform those services, practices, and responsibilities consistent with the historic orthodox faith.

These responsibilities include:

1. Confronting false teaching.
2. Exercising church discipline.
3. Encouraging the "feeding of the flock."
4. Praying for the afflicted.
5. Screening and ordaining candidates for the ministry.

Selection of Elders

The procedure for selecting elders is not an election. The procedure is a process of selection under the guidance of the Holy Spirit. The role of the congregation is to identify and communicate to the existing elder board potential candidates for eldership. The role of the elder board is to prayerfully investigate, qualify, and select candidates to become new elders. The congregation celebrates the completion of the process with affirmation of the new elders at an exaltation celebration.

ELDER SELECTION DETAILS

The selection committee consists of the existing elder board. The vice chairman of the elder board shall be responsible for ensuring the selection process is carried to completion. The selection process will begin in

June and end when the congregation, which should occur at an exaltation service in December, presents the nominees for affirmation. The
role of the Holy Spirit in this process must not be underestimated.

1. The vice chairman of the board shall ensure the nomination process begins at the appropriate time and continues smoothly to
   completion.
2. Prior to the start of the nominating process, announce the dates
   of the nomination period and explain the procedure and qualifications for selection of new elders in the church newsletter. This
   will commence in June.
3. For a period of approximately thirty days, the elder board will
   accept nominations from the congregation. This period will be
   known as the "nominating period." This will occur during the
   month of June.
   a. Nomination forms (see attached) will be made available in
      the church.
   b. Nominations must be placed inside a secure box. The vice
      chairman of the elder board shall arrange for the suitable
      care and custody of the nominations contained in the
      nomination box.
   c. A brief notice will be included in the church publication each
      week during the nominating period.
4. Prior to the July elder board meeting, the nominations will be
   unsealed and collated into a list by the vice chairman of the board
   and the secretary. This list of nominees will then be reviewed by
   the vice chairman of the board to ensure each of the nominees are
   male members of the church. The elder board at its July meeting
   shall review the list of candidates, and the name of any individual
   not qualified to serve as an elder shall be removed from the list.
   At least two elders must consent to the removal of any name from
   the list.
5. At least two orientation meetings shall be held before the end of
   August in order that each candidate may participate in one of
   the meetings. The meetings shall be mandatory for anyone who
   desires to continue in the selection process, and shall cover the
   roles and responsibilities of the elder board and individual elders,
   the selection process and the governance policy of the church.
   Candidates shall have the opportunity to ask questions during the
   meetings. Candidates shall have until September 1 to determine if
   they desire to continue in the selection process. Those continuing
   in the process shall be matched with current elders for a one-on-
   one meeting to answer other questions.

6. The elder board, at its July meeting, shall select a committee from the congregation. The committee shall be charged with conducting the initial interview of each of the candidates and providing a report to the elder board of the results of the interviews. A meeting shall be held with the committee by the chairman and vice chairman to explain the process as well as answer any questions the committee members may have before they begin the interview process.

   a. The committee shall be composed of members of [this church], of not less than three or more than five members, both men and women. They shall be known to be scripturally knowledgeable and demonstrate biblical wisdom and behavior in their lives. At least two alternates shall be named, who will be asked to serve if any of those originally named shall be unable or choose not to serve. At least one member of the committee shall be an ordained pastor of the church staff. The elders shall determine the chairperson of the committee with an alternate named.

7. The interview process and final report from the committee shall be completed and provided to the vice chairman of the elder board on or before October 10.

   a. At the elder board prayer meeting in October, copies of the committee's report shall be made available to each of the elders. Between then and the elder board prayer meeting of November, the elder board shall meet with and interview each of the candidates and their spouses.

   b. At the November prayer meeting, the elders shall make the final selection of nominees and cause their names to be included in the program for the next exaltation service or other appropriate church publication, but not later than November 15.

   c. A committee of at least two elders, one of whom should be the vice chairman, shall meet with candidates who were not selected for service as an elder. This meeting shall be held before the publication of the list of elder candidates.

8. The names of remaining candidates will be published in the church newsletter during the month of November, following completion of all interviews and affirmation of the elder board. This will introduce the candidates and invite written feedback from the congregation. In addition, other means of presenting the candidates to the congregation may be used, such as live or videotaped interviews for presenting at appropriate exaltation services.

a. All feedback from the congregation will be directed to the vice chairman of the elder board.

b. The elder board will evaluate feedback.

    i. If the negative feedback is deemed valid and warrants further investigation, an interview will be arranged with all parties involved.

    ii. If it is assumed frivolous criticism, it will be recognized for what it is.

9. The vice chairman of the elder board will notify new elders of their selection. The selections will be celebrated at the first possible exaltation service in December.

10. The three-year term of service of the new elders will commence January 1. The new elders will be invited, as a courtesy, to attend the December elder board meeting.

NOMINATION FORM INFORMATION

The procedure for selecting elders at [this church] is not an election. The procedure is a process of selection under the guidance of the Holy Spirit. The role of the congregation is to identify and communicate to the existing elder board potential candidates for eldership. The role of the elder board is to prayerfully investigate, qualify, and select candidates to become new elders. The completion of the process is celebrated by the congregation with the affirmation of the new elders at exaltation.

THE SCRIPTURAL CHARACTERISTICS OF ELDERS (1 TIM. 3:1–7 AND TITUS 1:5–9)

The husband of one wife

Not a lover of money

Self-controlled

Respectable

Hospitable

Able to teach

Not given to much wine

Not violent, but gentle

Temperate (not given to extremes)

Manages his family well

Not quarrelsome

Children obey him with respect

Not a recent convert

Good reputation with outsiders

Above reproach

SELECTION POLICY

Only men with the following qualifications will be considered.

1. Must be a member of record of [this church].
2. Able to demonstrate characteristics in his life that are delineated in the Scriptures as being characteristics of an elder.
3. A faithful giver.
4. There must be a one-year interval between terms for existing elders. (A list of current elders will be printed.)

Briefly answer the following questions:

Nominee's name _____

1. What positive characteristics would this candidate bring to the elder board?

2. I have prayerfully considered this nomination:

Nominator's name (optional) _____

Ordination and Licensing of Staff

BACKGROUND

The staff of [this church] is comprised of individuals who carry out a diverse variety of roles and responsibilities. Many have sensed the call of God to devote themselves to a vocation of Christian service, and these individuals are vital to the effectiveness of [this church's] ministry.

The elder board has determined that certain positions within the staff should be filled by ordained ministers. These individuals are authorized by the elder board to use the title of Reverend or Pastor with their name and job title, if they choose to do so.

There is another group of staff personnel who have accepted the special disposition to dedicate themselves to fulfilling pastoral roles in the church. As an integral and defined part of their job description, they are involved in teaching church members and attendees or youth and children. This group also participates in discipling leaders, providing biblical counseling, and managing programs that equip Christ-followers to develop their spiritual gifts and offer them in service to God. In addition, they may perform sacerdotal functions such as baptism and communion. These individuals may be certified/licensed by the elder board to perform the specific role that he or she has been employed to fill.

Thus there is only a small difference between the leadership staff and those serving in other church staff positions—that difference primarily being the professional religious training and/or corresponding practical experience and religious knowledge received by those who have been ordained.

A third group of staff employees are engaged in supporting roles, which may require, among other things, clerical skills, information systems skills, and facility maintenance skills. The training and job knowledge required by these individuals are not normally of a religious nature.

LOCAL ORDINATION REQUIREMENTS

There are two qualification categories for ordination at [this church]. Each case will be considered individually and judged on its own comprehensive merit, but the general requirements are as follows:

Category 1—Requirements for staff hired from within the congregation.

- A minimum of two years of experience in a position defined as a pastoral ministry.
- They shall demonstrate a vibrant, growing personal relationship with God and a commitment to serving him as a lifelong vocational career.
- They shall demonstrate an appropriate level of spiritual maturity and leadership.
- They shall show evidence of biblical knowledge and understanding befitting an ordained minister (roughly equivalent to a bachelor's degree in biblical studies).

Category 2—Requirements for a "Timothy" (i.e., a member who is ordained by our congregation and then sent out to minister elsewhere).

- A bachelor's degree in practical ministry, Bible, theology, etc. from an accredited Bible college or a postgraduate degree from a theological seminary.
- They shall demonstrate a vibrant, growing personal relationship with God and a commitment to serve him as a lifelong vocational career.
- They shall demonstrate an appropriate level of spiritual maturity and leadership.
- Personal knowledge of the individual and his/her family.

ORDINATION PROCESS

The process of reviewing a potential candidate for ordination will typically occur as follows:

- The candidate makes application to the board of elders.
- The senior pastor reviews the application and makes recommendation to the elder board.
- The elder board reviews and discusses the application and recommendation.
- Notification of candidate of selection/nonselection.
- Ceremony at an appropriate ordination service.

CERTIFICATION/LICENSING PROCESS

The process of reviewing a potential candidate for licensing/certification will typically occur as follows:

1. The individual is hired through the normal hiring process to fulfill a particular responsibility of the church staff. It would be expected that the individual hired would have the spiritual skills and knowledge, as well as the administrative skills necessary to fulfill the responsibilities of the job with minimal supervision and training.
2. The senior pastor makes recommendation to the elder board that the individual be certified/licensed.
3. The elder board considers the individual's leadership skills, job related abilities, and spiritual maturity as appropriate, and approves/disapproves the action requested.

Local Marriage Policy

[This church] is committed to building strong marriages, and we therefore want to do everything possible to help a man and a woman develop a solid foundation from the very beginning of their marriage commitment. We view the agreement to perform a wedding ceremony to be more of a partnership than a onetime event. Our responsibility in this partnership is to provide tools for building a strong marriage and to give clear direction concerning the scriptural guidelines that God has established for marriage.

We believe that God created the marriage covenant and he has given us basic principles and guidelines that will help us to experience joy and fulfillment in marriage. Application of these principles, in accordance with this policy, will help participants to have a wonderful wedding experience and increase the potential for a strong and growing marriage.

Accordingly, the following requirements for any man and woman desiring to be married in [this church] facility have been established.

1. A minimum of four months preparation time. This will allow time to complete the premarital counseling class. However, four months does not allow much time for a marriage in the midst of preparing for a wedding. Therefore, it is recommended that couples commit to a longer preparation time than the four-month minimum, if possible.

2. Regular attendance at [this church] during the four-month preparation time. If a meaningful partnership is to be developed between the wedding couple and the church family, it is important for the couple to know the church and what it stands for. Therefore, it is required that the couple attend a weekend service at least twice per month during the four-month preparation period.

3. Completion of the eight-week marriage preparation class. We believe this to be a valuable experience in developing tools for a lasting and fulfilling marriage.

4. If divorced, at least one year of legal divorce must pass before considering remarriage. A new relationship should not be pursued until the potential for a healthy reconciliation has been exhausted and time for personal healing and recovery has passed (1 Cor. 7:10–11).

5. A believer should only marry another believer. Scripture is very clear that those who have given their lives to Christ and live in authentic relationship with him should not be joined together with someone who has not also been transformed by Jesus Christ. For this reason we will not conduct a wedding that joins a Christian together with a non-Christian (1 Cor. 7:39; 2 Cor. 6:14–16; 1 John 5:1–5).

6. Commitment to sexual purity prior to marriage. Couples who are living together or who are currently involved in physical re-

lationships must be willing to separate and abstain from sexual intimacy until after marriage. The principle of maintaining sexual purity prior to marriage is defined very clearly in Scripture (1 Cor. 6:18–20; 1 Thess. 4:3–8).

7. The choice to follow these guidelines in order to be married at [this church] is up to each couple. The church believes these guidelines will be highly beneficial to any marriage relationship. Thus the church will not only adhere to them, but will also strongly recommend they be followed even if a couple decides during counseling they will be married elsewhere.

Note: If a couple believes they have extenuating circumstances regarding any aspect of this marriage policy, they should express their situation and concerns in writing to the chairman of the elder board. He will take the information to the elder board for resolution. A committee may be formed to meet with the couple for further discussion and resolution.

Resolving Conflict

[This church's] bylaws require that the elders be responsible for discipline within the church. This will be handled on a case-by-case basis, using Scripture as the guide.

After ensuring that all informal levels have been taken, the elder board will take the following steps:

STEP 1

a. Assign someone to document the proceedings from this point on so that they can be reviewed if similar situations should occur in the future. There must be consistency in how these situations are dealt with. Every effort should be made to be impartial.

b. The chairman of the elders will assign a committee of three impartial elders to meet with the offended party and evaluate the severity of the situation. These elders will preside over the matter until it is resolved. At this level there must be total confidentiality and neither side should be considered right or wrong prior to investigating. ("The first to present his case seems right, till another comes forward and questions him," Prov. 18:17.)

c. The elder committee will meet with the offending party and attempt to reach a satisfactory solution. The goal, of course, is to help both parties deal with the conflict in a manner that reconciles their differences and guides them back to unity with each other and the body of Christ.

d. If no satisfactory solution can be reached, the elders assigned to investigate the matter will proceed to the next step.

STEP 2

a. Take the matter to the full board of elders. The elders will act according to what Jesus taught about handling a person who refuses to reconcile with a brother or sister in Christ (Matt. 18:17).

b. Taking the matter to the elders, who represent the church, will generally be all that is necessary. But if the situation is severe enough, the elders will meet with those in the church body that they feel need to know about the situation. This might be a small group of people involved in ministry with the recalcitrant party. But even though it is not very likely, it is conceivable that some situations might justify taking it to the entire congregation. This might involve a person attempting to defraud members of the congregation at large or a person whose behavior poses a physical or emotional danger to people.

STEP 3

When all efforts to restore an erring brother or sister have failed, the elders must proceed with formal expulsion from the church. However unpleasant, this action was recommended by the apostle Paul when the severity of one man's sin called for it (". . . put out of your fellowship the man who did this," 1 Cor. 5:2b).

Note: There are two levels of expulsion:

Level one: The expelled person is removed from membership and not allowed to serve in a ministry or leadership role of any kind. By the same token, in keeping with the church's open invitation for lost people to "come as you are, sins and all," this person would not be barred from attending church services.

Level two: The expelled person is removed from membership and not allowed on church property.

STEP 4

In time, when and if it seems appropriate, the elders will seek to reconcile the expelled party with the church, as Paul instructed in 2 Corinthians 2:5–11. This must be undertaken with care so as not to trivialize the severity of the expelled person's offense, while at the same time demonstrating God's willingness to forgive erring people when they truly repent of their sins.

Scriptural Basis for the Church's Ends Policies

GLOBAL ENDS POLICY

Therefore go and make disciples of all nations, baptizing them in the name of the Father and of the Son and of the Holy Spirit, and teaching them to obey everything I have commanded you. And surely I am with you always, to the very end of the age.

Matthew 28:19–20

But you will receive power when the Holy Spirit comes on you; and you will be my witnesses in Jerusalem, and in all Judea and Samaria, and to the ends of the earth.

Acts 1:8

All this is from God, who reconciled us to himself through Christ and gave us the ministry of reconciliation: that God was reconciling the world to himself in Christ, not counting men's sins against them. And he has committed to us the message of reconciliation.

2 Corinthians 5:18–19

It was he who gave some to be apostles, some to be prophets, some to be evangelists, and some to be pastors and teachers, to prepare God's people for works of service, so that the body of Christ may be built up until we all reach unity in the faith and in the knowledge of the Son of God and become mature, attaining to the whole measure of the fullness of Christ.

Ephesians 4:11–13

For Christ died for sins once for all, the righteous for the unrighteous, to bring you to God. He was put to death in the body but made alive by the Spirit.

1 Peter 3:18

STRATEGIC PURPOSE

They devoted themselves to the apostles' teaching and to the fellowship, to the breaking of bread and to prayer. . . . They broke bread in their homes and ate together with glad and sincere hearts, praising God and enjoying the favor of all the people. And the Lord added to their number daily those who were being saved.

Acts 2:42, 46–47

I have not hesitated to preach anything that would be helpful to you but have taught you publicly and from house to house.

Acts 20:20

For those God foreknew he also predestined to be conformed to the likeness of his Son, that he might be the firstborn among many brothers.

Romans 8:29

Do not conform any longer to the pattern of this world, but be transformed by the renewing of your mind. Then you will be able to test and approve what God's will is—his good, pleasing and perfect will.

Romans 12:2

Be devoted to one another in brotherly love.

Romans 12:10

Let us not give up meeting together, as some are in the habit of doing, but let us encourage one another—and all the more as you see the Day approaching.

Hebrews 10:25

EVANGELISM

Therefore go and make disciples of all nations, baptizing them in the name of the Father and of the Son and of the Holy Spirit.

Matthew 28:19

For God so loved the world that he gave his one and only Son, that whoever believes in him shall not perish but have eternal life.

John 3:16

For the wages of sin is death, but the gift of God is eternal life in Christ Jesus our Lord.

Romans 6:23

All this is from God, who reconciled us to himself through Christ and gave us the ministry of reconciliation: that God was reconciling the world to himself in Christ, not counting men's sins against them. And he has committed to us the message of reconciliation.

2 Corinthians 5:18–19

He saved us, not because of righteous things we have done, but because of his mercy. He saved us through the washing of rebirth and renewal by the Holy Spirit.

Titus 3:5

EXALTATION

I will praise you, O LORD, with all my heart.

Psalm 9:1

Delight yourself in the LORD and he will give you the desires of your heart.

Psalm 37:4

Praise the LORD. Praise God in his sanctuary; praise him in his mighty heavens. Praise him for his acts of power; praise him for his surpassing greatness. Praise him with the sounding of the trumpet, praise him with the harp and lyre, praise him with tambourine and dancing, praise him with the strings and flute, praise him with the clash of cymbals, praise him with resounding cymbals. Let everything that has breath praise the LORD. Praise the LORD.

Psalm 150

Now all has been heard; here is the conclusion of the matter: Fear God and keep his commandments, for this is the whole duty of man.

Ecclesiastes 12:13

Jesus replied, "'Love the Lord your God with all your heart and with all your soul and with all your mind.' This is the first and greatest commandment."

Matthew 22:37–38 (Jesus is quoting Deuteronomy 6:5)

God is spirit, and his worshipers must worship in spirit and in truth.

John 4:24

EDIFICATION

We proclaim him, admonishing and teaching everyone with all wisdom, so that we may present everyone perfect in Christ.

Colossians 1:28

Like newborn babes, crave pure spiritual milk, so that by it you may grow up in your salvation, now that you have tasted that the Lord is good.

1 Peter 2:2–3

Therefore let us leave the elementary teachings about Christ and go on to maturity.

Hebrews 6:1

And this is my prayer: that your love may abound more and more in knowledge and depth of insight, so that you may be able to discern what is best and may be pure and blameless until the day of Christ.

Philippians 1:9–10

Let us therefore make every effort to do what leads to peace and to mutual edification.

Romans 14:19

Be imitators of God, therefore, as dearly loved children and live a life of love, just as Christ loved us and gave himself up for us.

Ephesians 5:1–2

Be devoted to one another in brotherly love.

Romans 12:10

Carry each other's burdens, and in this way you will fulfill the law of Christ.

Galatians 6:2

. . . teaching them to obey everything I have commanded you. And surely I am with you always, to the very end of the age.

Matthew 28:20

EXTENSION

Jesus replied: "'Love the Lord your God with all your heart and with all your soul and with all your mind.' This is the first and greatest commandment."

Matthew 22:37–38

Just as each of us has one body with many members, and these members do not all have the same function, so in Christ we who are many form one body, and each member belongs to all the others. We have different gifts, according to the grace given us. If a man's gift is prophesying, let him use it in proportion to his faith. If it is serving, let him serve; if it is teaching, let him teach; if it is encouraging, let him encourage; if it is contributing to the needs of others, let him give generously; if it is leadership, let him govern diligently; if it is showing mercy, let him do it cheerfully.

Romans 12:4–8

There are different kinds of gifts, but the same Spirit. There are different kinds of service, but the same Lord. There are different kinds of working, but the same God works all of them in all men.

1 Corinthians 12:4–6

The only thing that counts is faith expressing itself through love.

Galatians 5:6

You, my brothers, were called to be free. But do not use your freedom to indulge the sinful nature; rather, serve one another in love.

Galatians 5:13

It was he who gave some to be apostles, some to be prophets, some to be evangelists, and some to be pastors and teachers, to prepare God's people for works of service, so that the body of Christ may be built up until we all reach unity in the faith and in the knowledge of the Son of God and become mature, attaining to the whole measure of the fullness of Christ.

Ephesians 4:11–13

Each of you should look not only to your own interests, but also to the interests of others.

Philippians 2:4

Each one should use whatever gift he has received to serve others, faithfully administering God's grace in its various forms.

1 Peter 4:10

ENCOURAGEMENT

I tell you the truth, anyone who gives you a cup of water in my name because you belong to Christ will certainly not lose his reward.

Mark 9:41

Be devoted to one another in brotherly love.

Romans 12:10

Share with God's people who are in need. Practice hospitality.

Romans 12:13

Rejoice with those who rejoice; mourn with those who mourn.

Romans 12:15

Carry each other's burdens, and in this way you will fulfill the law of Christ.

> Galatians 6:2

Encourage the timid, help the weak, be patient with everyone.

> 1 Thessalonians 5:14

Encourage one another daily, as long as it is called Today, so that none of you may be hardened by sin's deceitfulness.

> Hebrews 3:13

Let us consider how we may spur one another on toward love and good deeds.

> Hebrews 10:24

Suppose a brother or sister is without clothes and daily food. If one of you says to him, "Go, I wish you well; keep warm and well fed," but does nothing about his physical needs, what good is it? In the same way, faith by itself, if it is not accompanied by action, is dead.

> James 2:15–17

Above all, love each other deeply, because love covers over a multitude of sins.

> 1 Peter 4:8

NOTES

Introduction

1. Aubrey Malphurs, *Being Leaders* (Grand Rapids: Baker, 2003); Aubrey Malphurs and Will Mancini, *Building Leaders* (Grand Rapids: Baker, 2004).

Chapter 1 Who Is Leading the Churches?

1. Carl S. Dudley and David A. Roozen, *Faith Communities Today: A Report on Religion in the United States Today*, online at http://fact.hartsem.edu/ (March 2001).

2. Randy Frazee with Lyle E. Schaller, *The Comeback Congregation* (Nashville: Abingdon, 1995), 11.

3. Win Arn, *The Pastor's Manual for Effective Ministry* (Monrovia, CA: Church Growth, 1988), 41.

4. Thom S. Rainer, "Shattering Myths about the Unchurched," *Southern Baptist Journal of Theology* 5:1 (Spring 2001): 47.

5. George Barna, *Leaders on Leadership* (Ventura, CA: Regal, 1997), 18.

6. John Carver, *Boards That Make a Difference* (San Francisco: Jossey-Bass, 1997), xiii, 19.

7. Ibid., 19.

8. Peter F. Drucker, *Management: Tasks, Responsibilities, Practices* (New York: Harper–Collins, 1974), 628.

9. Carver, *Boards That Make a Difference*, xiv.

10. George Babbes, "Ministries Mired in Mediocrity," online at http://www.regent.edu/review/v1n2/commentary (October 15, 2002), 1.

11. Charles C. Ryrie, *Nailing Down a Board* (Grand Rapids: Kregel, 1999), 9.

12. Ibid., 11.

13. James F. Bolt, "Developing Three-Dimensional Leaders," *Leader of the Future: New Essays by World-Class Leaders and Thinkers*, ed. Francis Hesselbein et al (San Francisco: Jossey-Bass, 1996), 163.

Chapter 2 The Governing Board

1. John Carver and Miriam M. Carver, *Reinventing Your Board* (San Francisco: Jossey-Bass, 1997), 167.

2. Lyle E. Schaller, *The Very Large Church: New Rules for Leaders* (Nashville: Abingdon, 2000), 115.

3. Colin B. Carter and Jay W. Lorsch, *Back to the Drawing Board* (Boston: Harvard Business School Press, 2004), 17.

4. Ibid., 89.

Chapter 5 Board Composition

1. The Carvers are very helpful in thinking through the responsibilities of the chairperson's role. See Carver and Carver, *Reinventing Your Board*, 103–4.

2. Carter and Lorsch, *Back to the Drawing Board*, 104.

3. Ryrie, *Nailing Down a Board*, 65.

4. Ibid., 66.

5. Aubrey Malphurs, *Doing Church* (Grand Rapids: Kregel, 1999).

6. Aubrey Malphurs, *Values-Driven Leadership*, 2d ed. (Grand Rapids: Baker, 2004).

Chapter 7 The Effective Board

1. Larry Osborne, *The Unity Factor* (Carol Stream, IL: Word, 1989), 66–68.

2. See my discussion of this in Malphurs, *Doing Church*, 16.

3. Charles Ryrie, *A Survey of Bible Doctrine* (Chicago: Moody, 1972).

Chapter 8 The Policies Approach to Governance

1. Aubrey Malphurs, *Advanced Strategic Planning* (Grand Rapids: Baker, 1999); and Aubrey Malphurs, *Ministry Nuts and Bolts* (Grand Rapids: Kregel, 1997).

2. Carver, *Boards That Make a Difference*, chapter 5.

3. Carver also covers this topic in chapter 5.

4. Glenn Parker, *Team Players and Teamwork* (San Francisco: Jossey-Bass, 1990).

Chapter 9 Board Policies

1. Carver, *Boards That Make a Difference*, 34.

2. Carver and Carver, *Reinventing Your Board*, 103.

3. Ibid., chap. 5.

4. Carver, *Boards That Make a Difference*, 107.

5. Ibid., chap. 5.

6. Ibid., 88–94.

7. Contact us at The Malphurs Group if you desire to pursue strategic planning and want a competent consultant to guide you through the process (amalphurs@dts.edu or www.malphursgroup.com).

Chapter 10 Board Meetings

1. Larry Bossidy and Ram Charan, *Execution: The Discipline of Getting Things Done* (New York: Crown Business, 2002), 102.

2. Patrick Lencioni, *The Five Dysfunctions of a Team* (San Francisco: Jossey-Bass, 2002).

Chapter 11 Implementing a Policies Approach

1. Again, The Malphurs Group can assist you with this.

Appendix J The Church and Power

1. Charles Ryrie, *A Survey of Bible Doctrine* (Chicago: Moody Press, 1972), 148.

Appendix K Skillman Bible Church Governance Policy

1. John Carver, *The Carver Guide Series on Effective Board Governance* (San Francisco: Jossey-Bass, 1996).

2. John Carver, *John Carver on Board Governance* (San Francisco: Jossey-Bass, 1993).

3. See John Carver, *Carver Guide No. 2: Your Roles and Responsibilities as a Board Member* (San Francisco: Jossey-Bass, 1997), 11–18.

4. See John Carver, *Carver Guide No. 5: Planning Better Board Meetings* (San Francisco: Jossey-Bass, 1997), 9–11.

5. Skillman Bible Church has a mission and vision statement formulated in the year prior to the study that led to this document. The principles given in this document are helpful as the board continues to hone the mission of the church.

6. See John Carver, *Carver Guide No. 8: Board Self-Assessment* (San Francisco: Jossey-Bass, 1997), 4–5.

7. See John Carver, *Carver Guide No.3: Three Steps to Fiduciary Responsibility* (San Francisco: Jossey-Bass, 1997), 10.

Sources

Biehl, B., and Ted Engstrom. *The Effective Board Member.* Nashville: Broadman, 1998.

Carver, John. *Carver Guide No. 1: Basic Principles of Policy Governance.* San Francisco: Jossey-Bass, 1997.

———. *Carver Guide No. 3: Three Steps to Fiduciary Responsibility.* San Francisco: Jossey-Bass, 1997.

———. *Carver Guide No. 4: The Chairperson's Role as the Servant Leader to the Board.* San Francisco: Jossey-Bass, 1997.

———. *Carver Guide No. 6: Creating a Mission That Makes a Difference.* San Francisco: Jossey-Bass, 1997.

———. *Carver Guide No. 7: Board Assessment of the CEO.* San Francisco: Jossey-Bass, 1997.

———. *Carver Guide No. 9: Making Diversity Meaningful in the Board-room.* San Francisco: Jossey-Bass, 1997.

———. *Carver Guide No. 10: Strategies for Leadership.* San Francisco: Jossey-Bass, 1997.

———. *Carver Guide No. 11: Board Members as Fund Raisers, Advisers and Lobbyists.* San Francisco: Jossey-Bass, 1997.

———. *Carver Guide No. 12: The CEO Role Policy Governance.* San Francisco: Jossey-Bass, 1997.

Carver, John, and Miriam M. Carver. *Reinventing Your Board.* San Francisco: Jossey-Bass, 1997.

Hesselbein, Francis. *Hesselbein on Leadership.* San Francisco: Jossey-Bass, 2002.

Hesselbein, Francis, and R. Johnston, ed. *On Creativity, Innovation, and Renewal.* A Drucker Foundation Lifebook. San Francisco: Jossey-Bass, 2002.

———, eds. *On Leading Change.* A Drucker Foundation Lifebook. San Francisco: Jossey-Bass, 2002.

Houle, C. *Governing Boards.* San Francisco: Jossey-Bass, 1997.

Kotter, John. *John P. Kotter on What Leaders Really Do.* Harvard Business Review Book, Boston: Harvard Business School Press, 1999.

Oliver, C., ed. *The Policy Governance Field Handbook.* San Francisco: Jossey-Bass, 1999.

Ryrie, Charles. *Nailing Down a Board.* Grand Rapids: Kregel, 1999.

INDEX

Aubrey Malphurs is a visionary with a deep desire to influence a new generation of leaders through his classroom, pulpit, consulting, and writing ministries. He is involved in a number of other ministries ranging from church planting and growth to leadership development. He has pastored three churches and is the author of numerous books and articles on leadership and church ministry. Currently he is a professor at Dallas Theological Seminary, president of The Malphurs Group, and a trainer and consultant to churches, denominations, and ministry organizations throughout North America and Europe.